HOW THEY STARTED

Global Brands

How 21 good ideas became great global businesses

crimson

This edition first published in Great Britain in 2008 by
Crimson Publishing, a division of Crimson Business Ltd
Westminster House
Kew Road
Richmond
Surrey
TW9 2ND

A catalogue record for this book is available from the British Library.

ISBN 978 1 85458 447 2

Printed and bound by MPG Books Ltd, Bodmin

Contents

Introduction

This is our second *How They Started* book. The first was all about recently launched British businesses which made it. It did very well, and has led to lots of requests for this companion volume, focusing on some of the world's biggest global brands.

Many people are fascinated by how businesses that very often have been taken for granted as part of our lives actually began. Some of the people who have contacted us about the first book are entrepreneurs themselves, at various stages, but by no means all of them are. Others are people who have had an idea or two for a business but have never pursued it. And many are people who have become interested in starting companies as a result of the excellent TV programmes *The Apprentice* or *Dragons' Den*, and want to know more about what it really takes to get a business off the ground. They wonder whether they should have pursued their idea, whether they were cut out to be an entrepreneur, and enjoy the thoughts reading *How They Started* provokes.

And be under no illusion: reading this book will provoke thoughts. It is fascinating to learn why some of the products we take for granted actually came about. Just how much was carefully planned, and how much happened by pure chance? It's intriguing to wonder how things might have been without some of those twists of fate. And to wonder what might have become of some of your own ideas. Or whether there is another brilliant idea for a brand-new global business within your reach if you could just think a little more about it. I have started a number of successful businesses myself, and still get the same buzz of excitement from reading these stories; is there another great business I could start that would grow to this level of success?

One factor that makes this more tantalising than ever is the speed at which some businesses can grow. Google and Bebo are the two most obvious examples from this collection. Ten years ago, neither had been launched to 'consumers' yet today each has tens, or hundreds, of millions of people using them regularly. I am sure that in 10 years' time, there will be several more businesses that are as well known as Google is today which haven't been started yet. That's the nature of the world we live in, with technology speeding up the rate at which some businesses can grow. Could one of those new businesses be yours?

Whatever your reasons for reading this book, I hope it delivers what you want. Should it inspire you to go on and set up your own business, then wonderful – you have chosen a challenging but potentially very rewarding path. And should it put you off the idea, then well done for realising that perhaps being an entrepreneur isn't for you; it certainly isn't for everyone. One study I read recently suggests that roughly one in 20 people have the personality type to be an entrepreneur; no more.

HOW **THEY** STARTED

So, what does it take to be an entrepreneur, judging from the people whose stories are told in these pages? Two significant qualities rise above the rest: passion for the idea, and the determination to find a way through no matter what problems are encountered. Age, experience, family background and starting capital are not requirements – it is genuinely possible to build a truly great business whatever your current financial status, or age, or education level. As it should be.

How did we select the companies for this book?

We set out to find a wide variety of businesses, focusing on the sort of businesses most people think about starting, in other words avoiding less-practical ideas such as mining or financial institutions! From there, we applied three strict criteria:

- Most importantly, every company we cover was started by one or more individuals who had an idea.
- Every business we cover here is successful.
- They are all also a 'household name' in many countries around the world.

Above all, we wanted to show that good ideas, turned into businesses by one or a small group of people, have gone on to become global giants throughout the last 100 years or so, and continue to do so.

Wherever possible we have spoken to the founders directly; inevitably, given the age of some of the businesses covered here, some of those are dead, so we have relied on company archives and others who know the story.

It is a sad truth that very few of these companies were founded by women. The closest we get is Bebo, co-founded by Xochi Birch, Green & Black's, co-founded by Josephine Fairley, Lonely Planet, co-founded by Maureen Wheeler, and eBay, where a woman, Meg Whitman, was the CEO who drove most of eBay's substantial growth. Equally disappointing is the racial mix of founders, being predominantly white. Both of these have much to do with the era when the majority of the businesses covered, which is probably inevitable when trying to cover a group of such dominant brands, given when most of these were set up. About half the businesses we cover were started before the Second World War; and many more in the two decades after it ended, it would be the 1970s before women and non-white racial groups started to set up ambitious businesses, a trend which has grown far too slowly for many people's taste. I look forward to doing a new edition of *How They Started* in 10 years' time, and hopefully seeing a much wider variety of founders then.

While the majority of founders were aged between 25 and 40, there are exceptions at both ends of the age spectrum which prove age need not be a barrier. Pizza Hut was founded by college students, while its fast-food sibling KFC was founded by Harlan Sanders at the ripe old age of 56.

We set out to find a collection of companies founded all over the world. Inevitably this is biased towards the more developed 'western' economies which started far earlier than Asian and even east European businesses. Looking at a list of the largest global companies would yield a similar mix to that included within this book. Again, in 10 years' time, a new edition *How They Started* would feature considerably more Asian companies; one or two from Russia or central Europe, and possibly one or two from Brazil, given the nature and speed at which the global economy is changing.

What can we learn from these businesses as a group?

Why did they start?

Founders' motivations often play a significant role in the subsequent success (or failure) of a venture. Specifically, it is very rare for a business to succeed that is founded by someone whose passion is just to make their fortune. The businesses we profile here would support this – none were set up by someone just keen to make big bucks. The majority were founded by people who were passionate about their product – whether that be to improve something fundamentally, as in the cases of Google or Dyson, or simply because the founder loved an area so much that he wanted to work on it, as with Sony or Cloudy Bay. Interestingly, in all cases this passion for the product or service was combined with a clear belief that the fledgling business would be able to make enough money to survive; this was not mad-scientist passion with no regard for business reality.

Of the rest, a few were started by people who simply wanted to make a living; I especially like Pizza Hut's beginnings, where its founders simply wanted to pay their way through university. Volvo and Nokia, interestingly both Scandinavian, were founded in order to produce a certain type of product/introduce a particular process to the founders' home country. Nintendo's founder stands apart from the rest: Hiroshi Yamauchi inherited a tiny family firm in post-war Japan, and even before he agreed to take on the leadership role, he was determined that he would run it his way. He had no idea then that computer games would be the company's future, but was driven by ambition grounded, it seems, in honour, to look after and grow the family business which had been entrusted to him. I imagine his family are rather more than satisfied with the results.

How did they fund their growth?

The initial funding for all these businesses came from the founders themselves, with just two exceptions (Volvo and Nintendo). Very rapidly, though, many of these businesses took on business angel or venture capital funds, and more than half floated on stock exchanges to raise money for continued growth. The financial markets have worked well for this group of businesses.

Coca-Cola developed a novel way of funding its very rapid early growth – by licensing its product to bottlers in different territories. Later, Pizza Hut and KFC both used similar methods, pioneering the franchising system which is used by thousands of businesses as a way to grow using other people's money, effort and passion.

Of all the businesses featured here, Dyson is the business that struggled the most to raise capital. Yet you can understand those who turned it down – would you want to back a passionate inventor who wants to enter a market up against several well-established global giants? Venture capitalists naturally like to back growth sectors, and before Dyson, the vacuum cleaner market was regarded as mature.

IKEA stands out for its rigorous determination to remain privately held, which it believes has been crucial for its growth and success. This provides an interesting contrast in approach to the other stories here.

What does it take to succeed internationally?

To found a successful business in any country is a tremendous achievement. There are countless tales of businesses, successful in their home country, expanding abroad with disastrous consequences. At the time of writing there is very public scepticism among the business press about the likely success of British supermarket Tesco's expansion into the USA. Very often successful businesses don't travel well. So what have the businesses profiled here done right that sets them apart from the crowd?

All have focused on their international markets. For those founded in smaller economies, which included Japan at the time of founding for both Sony and Nintendo, exporting was viewed from an early stage as necessary for medium to long-term survival. And founders of successful businesses do whatever it takes to make their businesses survive; in many of the businesses here that meant international success.

In every case, products were either designed from the beginning for each particular export market, or adapted for each country, using local people to feed in that knowledge. The formula for success appears easy, though in most cases implementing it well is very far from easy: research local needs, launch a product tailored to that market, commit proper resources to the launch.

First-mover advantage

It is often said that the first entrant to market has significant advantage, able to build market share and brand loyalty without significant competition. Interestingly, roughly one third of our businesses profiled were the first to market with their product; businesses like Coca-Cola, Pizza Hut and Billabong. But two thirds were not. Bebo and Google have both grown enormously fast despite being up against considerable established competition, which they both overcame with better products extremely quickly. Dyson is perhaps the best example of the first movers becoming complacent and allowing a young upstart business to come from nowhere and take the market-leading position in most countries by delivering a clear product advantage.

What lessons can be drawn from this? To be first in the market can be a great advantage, but it is more important to be better than to be first. Success in business all over the world really does seem to come down to giving customers what they want, not just when you start, but continually.

David Lester
September 2008

≡ adidas®

adidas

A SPORTING SUCCESS

Founder: Adolf (Adi) Dassler

Age of founder at start: 20

Background: Trained as a baker

Year of foundation: 1949

Business type: Sporting goods company

Countries now trading in: Over 170

Sales and net profit: €10.3bn and €55lm (adidas Group 2007)

HOW **THEY STARTED**

A ny runner will tell you that the right shoes are key to success and it is this thinking that has been the driving force behind sporting goods manufacturer adidas. The company's origins go back nearly a century when one man, Adi Dassler was determined to provide every athlete with the best possible equipment. Today, the adidas Group is the world's second biggest sports equipment manufacturer with products ranging from footwear to clothing to accessories, focusing on running, football, basketball and training. It also possesses one of the world's most iconic brands, a distinctive logo of three stripes.

Inspiration leads to new shoes

German-born Adolf Dassler, nicknamed Adi, was an avid sportsman with a passion for extreme sports, having even built his own ski jump. A keen runner as well, he, like many other entrepreneurs, spotted a gap in the market – the need for better shoes – ones that enhanced performance and went beyond functionality. Adi had originally trained as a baker but he had a heritage steeped in shoes as his father was a cobbler. With a vision to produce the ideal sports shoe, it seemed his destiny to follow in his father's footsteps. In 1920 he started making sports shoes in his home town of Herzogenaurach, a small German village about 12 miles west of Nuremberg, with his mother's kitchen doubling as a workshop.

Germany after the First World War, however, was a tough place to start a business but Adi was determined not to let this stop him. He used whatever items he could scavenge to make his shoes, including parachutes and army helmets, while his sisters cut patterns out of canvas. Such creativity and sheer hard graft kept the business going, as well as Adi's vision to develop the perfect running shoe. This vision encompassed three guiding principles: produce the best shoe for the requirements of the job, protect the athlete from injury and ensure the product lasted.

In 1924 his brother Rudolf, who had a background in sales, joined Adi, and his venture into shoe making became a business. Rudolf became mainly responsible for the marketing side of the business, while Adi persevered with his shoe designs. The company name, Dassler Brothers Shoe Factory, was registered in the same year. By then, a handful of employees had joined the business in an expanded workshop, producing 50 pairs of shoes per day.

Adi's vision encompassed three guiding principles: produce the best shoe for the requirements of the job, protect the athlete from injury and ensure the product lasted

8

ADI DASSLER IN AN EARLY SHOE-MAKING FACTORY

Early growth

Adi, however, had already set his sights on bigger things and wanted to produce further technical innovations for the shoe. A year later he obtained his first patents: one for a running shoe and the other for a football boot. Shoes were designed for soccer and track and field and were lighter and sturdier than other available makes. Ever the perfectionist, Adi had even ensured that different running shoes were tailored for different distances, by testing them himself.

Interest picked up through word-of-mouth marketing as Adi always made time to attend important sporting events in Germany. He initially sold shoes to sports clubs and athletes, before expanding to supply footwear to participants at the 1928 Olympic games in Amsterdam, and at the same event held in Los Angles four years later. In 1931, the company's range of tennis shoes was launched and by the mid 1930s, Adi was making 30 different pairs of shoes for 11 types of sport, and employee numbers swelled to almost 100.

But it was the Olympics held in Adi's home country, the 1936 Berlin games, that proved pivotal to the company's development. By this time, Dassler shoes were worn by the majority of German athletes, and the brothers had realised that athletes themselves were the best advertisement for their products. It was therefore crucial to gain the endorsement of the top celebrated sporting people to generate a buzz around the brand. In fact, Adi became the first entrepreneur to use sports promotion to raise awareness of his products.

Kitting out the national athletic team with Dassler shoes was simply the beginning. True to his entrepreneurial flair, Adi took a risk and drove to the Olympic village with a suitcase full of his products, in an attempt to persuade US sprinter Jesse Owens to try Dassler shoes. The gamble paid off when Owens won four Olympic gold medals, sealing the firm's reputation among the world's elite athletes. Orders poured in from other teams and around 200,000 pairs of shoes were sold every year over the next three years, leading Adi to purchase a second production facility in 1938 to cope with the demand.

Adi became the first entrepreneur to use sports promotion to raise awareness of his products

Family split

The outbreak of the Second World War almost put paid to the business as the factory was seized by the military while Rudolf and most of the other employees were drafted into the army. Adi remained with the business, manufacturing products for the German army. After the war, with much of the country looking to rebuild and regroup, he continued to make sports shoes, but this time with a much smaller workforce of just under 50, although the local townspeople were keen to help out with the business as much as possible. Adi's creative flair again came to the fore, as he made shoes from a variety of materials leftover from the war, such as discarded military tents, leather baseball mitts and canvas and rubber from US fuel tanks.

As the business had developed though, the brothers had become increasingly at odds with each other, so much so that in 1948, they decided to part ways after yet another dispute. This split marked the start of a bitter rivalry centred on the shoe business as Rudolf took half of the company's shoe-making machines and started another shoe business across the river from his brother's. The company eventually became Puma, one of adidas' fiercest rivals.

With Adi in sole charge of the business, a new name was necessary. The word adidas was coined – a combination of his nickname and the first few letters of his last name, and the company name was officially registered in 1949. A new logo was designed to complement the name change, and Adi devised the now-iconic three-stripe design (which he had first thought of eight years earlier), creating a striking, visual image that aimed to make his shoes stand out from the crowd. The stripes were also there for practical reasons as they helped to support the arch of the foot. In that same year, Adi decided to focus his efforts on football shoes and produced his first shoes with moulded rubbers studs.

Sports promotion

Past experience had taught both brothers the importance of getting athletes to wear their products, and in many ways, the rivalry of the adidas and Puma brands marked the beginning of the concept of sports promotion and endorsement that exists today. Both worked hard to secure the backing of prominent athletes, particularly at the Olympic games, even resorting to handing out envelopes with cash. Adidas was the most widely worn German sports shoe brand at the Helsinki games in 1952, and marked the first time track shoes with removable spikes were used. The business also expanded its product range for the first time by introducing sports bags.

It was Adi who gained the crucial advantage in the adidas-Puma battle, when adidas kitted out the entire German national football team in 1954. The shoes had screw-in studs – a new feature for the time, compared to the standard moulded pattern. The company became the talk of the town when against the odds, West Germany won against Hungary – the final was played on a wet and rainy day and the shoes with screw-in studs proved to be a winner. Adi was featured in many newspapers along with the German players and the shoes came to the world's attention. In total, 450,000 pairs of shoes were produced in that year.

Such aggressive publicity became a standard feature of the company's strategy in the following years. Adidas came up with a product innovation for every major event, dominating the world's athletic shoe market and overtaking canvas trainers from the likes of Keds. Key to this aggressive growth was the fact that Adi was in constant contact with many of the world's elite athletes from a variety of disciplines, enabling him to perfect different shoes for a variety of sports.

adidas came up with a product innovation for every major event, dominating the world's athletic shoe market

HOW THEY STARTED

ADI WITH HIS PERFECTED FOOTBALL BOOTS WITH SCREW-IN STUDS

Global expansion

One example of this specialised design was the 1956 Olympics in Melbourne. Keeping things in the family, Käthe Dassler, Adi's wife and business partner, sent their son Horst to Australia to distribute adidas shoes to athletes competing in the event. In the book *Olympic Turnaround* (Michael Payne, Praeger Publishers Inc 2006), Horst is quoted as recalling how 'athletes were surprised when I came up, as a young chap and offered them a pair of shoes. It was very easy'.

Around the same time, Adi signed his first licensee agreement with a Norwegian shoe factory, ensuring that adidas was on the road to global expansion. Horst's involvement in the company grew and three years later, in 1959, he helped to establish and build production facilities in France, as well as setting up an additional factory in Germany. Taking the products to the athletes at the Melbourne games had been a shrewd move – at the games held in Rome in 1960, 75% of all track and field athletes were wearing adidas shoes.

Global expansion was matched by new product lines as adidas continued to push the boundaries of innovation. In the mid-1960s Adi and Käthe decided to move into the leisure and clothing sector, producing apparel for competition and training. The first adidas tracksuits with the three stripes logo were introduced in 1962 and ball production began in 1963. Celebrity endorsements continued to be one of the company's strengths, with both Muhammad Ali and Joe Frazier sporting special boxing shoes designed by Adi in the 1971 boxing match dubbed the 'Fight of the Century'. A year later, the three stripes logo was adapted to a trefoil (three-leaved plant) logo.

An ailing business

While the 1960s and early 1970s were marked by innovation, the latter part of this decade was marred by Adi's death in 1978. Rudolf had died some four years earlier, and the brothers had never reconciled their differences. By the time of Adi's death, the business had amassed 700 patents and other industrial property rights – proof of Adi's never-ending quest for the perfect shoe. Käthe continued to run the business, which by the time of Adi's death was producing a staggering 45 million pairs of shoes a year.

Käthe passed away six years later, and Horst assumed control of the business in 1985, but not before a major blunder had been made: the business turned down a trainer endorsement from a young Michael Jordan in 1984. Horst, however, had ambitious plans for a global restructure of the business, but tragically died three years later from cancer, aged 51, before his ideas could be put into action. Without a leader, adidas was heading towards an uncertain future. Earlier family feuds that had affected the business were resurrected as Adi's remaining four daughters squabbled over the company's future, causing adidas to lose direction and market share.

Competition and weak advertisement campaigns also played their part, with the likes of Nike and other brands flooding the sports shoe market, trouncing adidas time and time again and capturing ever-increasing slices of the North American market. Adidas' credentials as a family business came to an abrupt end in 1989, when the daughters sold the business for £320m ($512m) – considered a bargain at the time and equating to something like £573m ($1bn) today – to French businessman Bernard Tapie, who specialised in rescuing ailing businesses. Tapie, who later became Urban Affairs Minister in France, instigated a few changes, such as the launch of Equipment, a range of performance-oriented and functional footwear and clothing. Production was also moved offshore to Asia in an attempt to cut costs. But Tapie was unable to revive adidas' fortunes due to his own financial difficulties and he stepped down just a few years later, dogged by political and financial scandals.

In 1992, French bank Credit Lyonnais secured another buyer for adidas, which by this time was haemorrhaging more than £56m ($100m) a year and was heading towards bankruptcy, barely clinging on to a 3% share of the market. The new buyer, Harvard MBA graduate Robert Louis Dreyfus, had an enviable track record of business turnarounds. He took over in 1993, and together with a business partner, bought 15% of adidas – each investor reportedly paid £6,000 ($10,000), with banks and other investors stumping up the rest of the capital.

HOW **THEY** STARTED

The Dassler association with shoes hadn't quite come to an end though. Adi Dassler's grandson, who also shared the same first name, proved that shoes are certainly in the family's blood, when he founded shoe company AD One in 1992, specialising in adventure and suburban footwear.

Acquisitions and flotation

Dreyfus wasted no time putting his mark on the business. In adidas, he saw a company that had the ability to make fabulous shoes but which lacked the skills to sell them. He emphasised the firm's roots as a sports specialist, started to target a younger market, sacked most of the senior management and outsourced production to slash costs further, all the while investing heavily in marketing spend.

Acquisitions were also a part of adidas' comeback plan. In the same year that Dreyfus took over, the company bought a US sports marketing company called Sports Inc, renaming it adidas America and putting two former Nike executives in charge. It signalled that adidas was ready to take on Nike in its own backyard. It also took advantage of retro fashion trends at the time, relaunching a line of classic, old-school trainers that proved to be an instant hit, again firing a warning to Nike, whose focus at the time was on hi-tech innovation.

As part of its comeback plan, adidas took advantage of retro fashion trends at the time, relaunching a line of classic, old-school trainers that proved to be an instant hit

Flotation beckoned on the German and French stock exchange in 1995, masterminded by Dreyfus and further acquisitions followed. adidas even scored on the music scene when rapping group Run DMC wrote a song called *My adidas* in 1996, which later became one of the company's promotional songs. In 1997, adidas acquired French specialist ski-wear business Salomon Group and its subsidiary the TaylorMade Golf Company, expanding its offering into the sports equipment area. The business changed its name to adidas-Salomon and opened its first retail outlet in Portland, Oregon.

Road to recovery

By the time of its 50th anniversary in 1999, adidas had something to celebrate, not least the fact that its sales exceeded £3bn ($5bn) for the first time, with nearly 13,000 employees worldwide. A year later, adidas had become the official supplier and licensee of the Euro 2000 Football Championships. The following year, Herbert Hainer, formerly the deputy chairman and chief operating officer of the business, succeeded Dreyfus in the role of chief executive officer. By this time, adidas' identity was one that boasted a classy heritage alongside sports expertise. Further stores were opened in Tokyo, Berlin, Amsterdam and Paris, followed by New York in 2002 and Korea a year later. Initial results seemed promising, with the business achieving a 15% increase in earnings per share.

In that same year, adidas made some radical changes to the business, with the aim of expanding its customer base and increasing growth. Three new divisions were introduced, under the names of 'Sport Performance', 'Sport Heritage' and 'Sport Style', which combined a mixture of retro styles and fashion spin-offs. Two years later, adidas continued to make its name in the world of sports sponsorship, with sporting starts such as David Beckham and Tim Henman endorsing the brand. 2005 proved to be a busy year: a deal with fashion designer Stella McCartney to create a women's sports range for the brand was announced and adidas also announced the acquisition of US sports shoe rival Reebok in a deal worth £1.9bn ($3.8bn). (The Reebok acquisition was completed in 2006.) In May 2005, it announced the sale of its Salomon division to Finnish sports equipment firm Amer Sport and the business reverted back to the name adidas.

The company had made a name for itself in the past with technical innovations and the future was to be no different. In that same year, it launched the adidas 1, branded 'the world's first intelligent shoe', which boasted an in-sole computer to adjust heel cushioning in real time depending on changes in the running surface. Retailing at

A CLASSIC ADIDAS SHOE, ANTELOPE, WITH THE COMPANY'S TRADEMARK STRIPES

£125 ($250), it was certainly not cheap, priced at more than 50% above the next most expensive trainer on the market.

Where are they now?

Most recently, adidas has expanded its stores to major cities such as New York and London, as well as capitalising on opportunities in emerging markets like China or Russia. As well as being the Official Sportswear Partner at the Beijing 2008 Olympic games, it opened its largest store worldwide in Beijing in the run-up to the Olympics. It occupies four floors and has been called a 'Brand Centre', featuring products from the Performance and Style divisions. The purchase of Reebok, however, has yet to live up to expectations, and adidas admitted it 'still has a way to go' in its latest set of financial results released in August 2008. Reebok's growth has been hampered by sluggish sales in North America, the UK and Japan but future plans include increased targeting of the women's fitness market, with a women's-only product due to roll out next year. The Adidas Group is the second largest sporting goods company in the world after Nike but remains the leading brand in Europe, and is number one worldwide for sports apparel. It seems quite fitting then, that brand adidas' slogan is 'Impossible is Nothing'.

Billabong

FASHIONING THE NEXT WAVE

Founder: Gordon Merchant

Age of founder at start: 28

Background: Avid surf fan and worked as a surf board shaper

Year of foundation: 1973

Business type: Surfing fashion and accessories

Countries now trading in: 100

Turnover: £609m ($1bn)

HOW **THEY** STARTED

Surfing is a sport enjoyed by many and performed with differing degrees of success. Surfing is cool. But to be cool you also have to have the look to match. Surfing fashion is an important part of its appeal and has recently gone mainstream. Many people who are far from expert wave riders like to wear it and it can now be found everywhere: from the beach shops and surfing hire centres, to retailers in big cities in the most landlocked of areas. Billabong is the Australian company which, probably more than any other, propelled surf wear towards the high street. It is one of the most popular brands and even after over 35 years of trading it is still one of the biggest labels in the industry, second only to Australian-founded but US-owned Quiksilver. It is one of the big reasons why we can find items such as surf shorts in most major cities. However, it was an uphill battle for the company from the outset and for years it wasn't taken seriously by banks and financial institutions. Its founder Gordon Merchant demonstrated great determination in his quest for success. The dedication which he displayed in the face of rejection has now paid off handsomely. Gordon is one of Australia's most successful entrepreneurs, a millionaire many, many times over. His company, which is listed on Australian Securities Exchange, is valued at A$2.7bn (£1.2bn/$2.2bn).

The coming wave

Gordon Merchant loves surfing. Even today, as a man in his 60s, he still spends as much time as possible hunting and riding the best waves in Australia. During the early 1970s, he spent all his free time surfing. He was so in love with the ocean that the Maroubra-bred man moved permanently to Burleigh Heads on the Gold Coast of Australia, where he could spend nine months of every year riding the big swells.

Gordon worked as a surfboard shaper looking for ways to perfect a board that would provide the ultimate ride. He made several innovations which have helped transform the industry. The first was the leg rope which, as any surfer who has spent precious time chasing after their board following a wipe-out knows, is one of the simplest yet most useful things ever added to a surfboard. Gordon also added the tucked-under edge which has helped some of Australia's finest surfers scale the heights of success. However, the chemicals used in the manufacture of surfboards were proving detrimental to Gordon's health and he wanted to move into something else. And, like many great entrepreneurial stories Gordon found his inspiration in the world in which he inhabited. This meant, of course, that he would create a business connected to his great love, surfing.

Gordon worked as a surfboard shaper . . . he made several innovations which have helped transform the industry

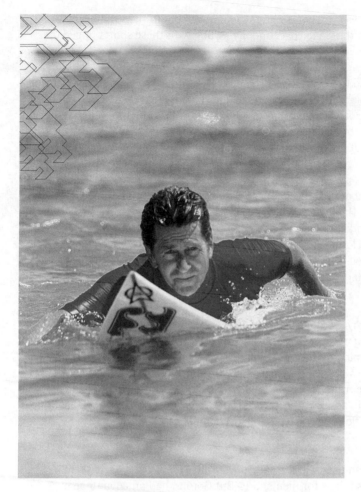

GORDON MERCHANT DOING WHAT HE LOVES BEST

Catching the swell

Gordon realised that there was a serious lack of good-quality, dedicated surf wear. The surf shops you see today on beaches across the world just didn't exist then. Surfers' clothing was dominated by menswear stores, but they didn't understand what surfers really needed and the shorts they sold were hopeless for surfing. 'They were made of cotton thread which rotted in saltwater and they never fitted properly,' Gordon recalls in the book *Only a Surfer Knows the Feeling: The Story of Billabong's Surfwear Revolution* (Derek Rielly, RollingYouth Press 2003). 'You'd feel like a real dork wearing them up to your belly button, and they would always creep up which made them uncomfortable.' Gordon remembers when he was at the Stubbies, the surfing world championship, and he saw Mark Richards deliberately tear his shorts up the sides in order to get the leg movement he needed. 'Mark Richards tore his board shorts up the side – it was the only way you could get any leg movement in them. I'll never forget the sight of him up on the stage collecting his trophy with these shorts ripped up the side.'

He knew something had to be done and that there was a great demand from surfers for boardshorts which could withstand the rigours of surfing. There were a number of other surf-wear makers but Gordon was unimpressed by their efforts and believed that they didn't appreciate what surfers really wanted. 'The mainstream menswear labels knew how to make clothes but they didn't know anything about the fashion or marketing of functional surf wear.'

Gordon also wanted to get out of board shaping and so the idea of making great boardshorts appealed. His friend and fellow surfer Tommy Moses worked as a tailor and the pair began working together making shorts for fun. 'I persuaded him to start his own label, Creme Clothing, it wasn't surf-specific clothing, we were just having fun making clothes we liked. There was no one else doing that at the time and I saw the success that he was starting to have. That was part of the inspiration for giving it a go myself.'

Unlike his friend Tommy, Gordon was not a trained tailor. However, entrepreneurs often manage to shrug off such setbacks and plough on toward success. Gordon dealt with his own shortcoming in the most direct way by simply taking a crash course in clothing design to learn the skills he needed to get started. Soon he and his wife Rena began designing and cutting shorts on their kitchen table. 'It took a lot of trial and error but we eventually designed a type of shorts which were durable and functional for surfing. I was just figuring it all out and attending a crash course in pattern design as I went.'

There was much trial and error in the early days while Gordon and Rena searched for the right materials to use for their shorts. But Gordon had an advantage over the menswear stores: he was a dedicated surfer and understood better than they did what was required for boardshorts to really work. Also, in those early days Gordon wasn't trying to create a global business, he was simply trying to make great shorts for him and his fellow surfers to wear.

Gordon began selling the shorts out of the back of his station wagon and into small stores. As sales began to take off Gordon and Rena realised that they could make a business. 'We reached this point where we just looked at each other and realised that we could actually make a pretty decent living out of this. We forgot about the house we wanted to buy because every cent we made need to be ploughed back into the company to grow. The business needed the money more than anything else did.'

Gordon had an advantage over the menswear stores: he was a dedicated surfer and understood better than they did what was required

Crucially, Gordon was able to make innovations in the design of boardshorts just like he was when he was making surfboards. Shorts used by surfers needed to sustain the rigours and strains of the sea's waves. So Gordon invented a new type of stitching which improved the durability of the shorts. They realised that they had the product and there was a clear market need. So what was also required was a brand name. A friend suggested Billabong which Gordon liked as it was both striking and unique to Australia. But neither Gordon nor Rena foresaw that it would become the global brand it is today. Their ambitions were much more modest; they just wanted to be able to buy a house. As it happened, that ambition had to be put on hold as profit was constantly ploughed back in to the business.

Choppy waters

Gordon spent much of the time between 1973 and 1975 slaving away late at night making shorts. In order to really scale up, Gordon's growing business needed finance. However, the banks weren't at all receptive and refused to take Billabong seriously at first. Clothing manufacturers were looked down upon, as were surfers. Gordon switched banks on no less than four occasions before he could find one that was willing to take his idea seriously. 'No one wanted to take you seriously as a surf-wear manufacturer. I remember going into the bank to get a loan for the company and they just laughed at me. Clothing was a nasty word for the banks as so many clothing makers went broke; and surfers were even worse.'

But Gordon refused to give up and kept the business going until eventually he got the finance together. He also expanded his range, moving into t-shirts and tank tops as well as continuing his line in boardshorts. After he felt that the brand was sufficiently established he took out some classified adverts in the surfing press and later bought more expensive display ads. The company slowly worked its way across the Gold Coast and across Australia's eastern seaboard. It took most of the 1970s, but by the end of the decade Billabong was truly a national company. Because of the lack of bank finance, Billabong didn't grow as fast as it could have done. But after doing well across Australia, international expansion beckoned.

A MEN'S T-SHIRT FROM THE 2008 RANGE

The next wave

With a strong presence in Australia, Gordon began to see international expansion as the next move. Australia is seen by many as the home of surfing and so the business felt that its very Australian Billabong brand would work well with consumers in surfing markets overseas. Looking north, they thought Japan would be a good territory for them, and the obviously lucrative, and notoriously difficult US market was also an area that Gordon wanted to move into. Foreign retailers were impressed by the impact that the company had made on its own home market and were therefore prepared to give Billabong products a trial. Later Billabong started to sell licences to foreign distributors overseas, which accelerated the company's expansion.

Foreign retailers were impressed by the impact that the company had made on its own home market

The company has always kept close ties with the surfing community. It runs its own surf competitions, including four of the 11 events on the men's World Championship Tour and two of the eight women's events and has maintained its Australian base. This is a smart marketing strategy as it ensures that the world's top surfers are all advocates of the Billabong brand. It serves to enhance the reputation of the company and means that newcomers to the sport are more likely to buy into it as they perceive it to be the best. Billabong's journey toward success was a long and slow one. The benefit to this was that there was never much temptation to try to make a fast buck at the expense of weakening the product. Now, after many years of hard work the company is unlikely to do anything that could limit its appeal.

Where are they now?

Gordon Merchant is still a part of Billabong's board and is one of Australia's most successful entrepreneurs. He still lives in Australia and despite being in his 60s he is still an avid surf fan. In fact, he has built himself a wave-shaped house in Angourie on the mid-north coast of New South Wales in Australia. He and Rena have now separated but Gordon still gives her the credit for much of the company's success, describing her as a tower of strength.

In 2000, Billabong floated on the Australian stock exchange. A consortium of backers bought a 49% stake in the company, effectively Rena's half. Billabong has used the market to make acquisitions and to enhance its profile as a global brand. In March 2001 Billabong acquired the Von Zipper sunglasses brand and, four months later, it purchased Element Skateboards. The successful integration of these businesses emboldened the company enough to bring several other brands under its umbrella; the Honolua Surf Company was acquired in January 2004 and Kustom footwear and Palmers Surf in September 2004.

The company has since continued its expansion, acquiring numerous other brands which form a part of the surfers' lifestyle. Nixon watches and accessories were added to the company in January 2006 and Element's footwear range and the California-based Beachworks retail business were introduced in 2007. The Group has also acquired the specialist wetsuit brand Xcel, girls swimwear brand Tigerlily and the US-based skateboard brand Sector 9 to bolster its brand portfolio.

Billabong has experienced almost tenfold growth since its flotation, with total sales up from approximately A$110m (£51.3m/$95.8m) in 1999 to more than $1bn in the 2005–2006 financial year. In the 2007-2008 financial year, profit increased by 12.6% in constant currency terms, and has announced another acquisition, the premium boardsport accessory brand DaKine.

Cloudy Bay

GROWING A VINTAGE BRAND

Founder: **David Hohnen**

Age of founder at start: **35**

Background: **Co-founded an Australian winery**

Year of foundation: **1984**

Age at foundation: **36**

Business type: **Winery**

Countries now trading in: **30**

Profit: **LVMH made £3bn ($5.2bn) (total for LVMH) from wines and spirits (2007)**

HOW **THEY** STARTED

Cloudy Bay is today probably the most famous white wine in the world. Yet Cloudy Bay's much-acclaimed Sauvignon Blanc propelled the company to international fame in only its second year of being. With an experienced and passionate winemaker at the helm, David Hohnen created something of a phenomenon when he sought out a New Zealand grape he had sampled in the mid-1980s. With a focus on quality, Cloudy Bay continued to make waves in the wine world, and was propelled on its way by a takeover in the early 1990s. The vineyard now crushes around 800 tonnes of grapes annually, working with six established contract growers over 200 hectares.

Rooted in wine

With a firm background in wine, David had started a Western Australian winery, Cape Mentelle, back in 1970 with his brother, Mark. David was not a novice at running a vineyard, indeed the entire Hohnen family was well versed in the art of wine. Their introduction to wine came when they lived in New Caledonia, where they were exposed to French culture and, of course, wine. The family then moved to Perth where a neighbour was running a small vineyard three hours south of the city. This looked appealing to the family, so in 1970, the Hohnens became the third family to plant vines in this now-famous region of Australia. This first company, Cape Mentelle, was run by David and his brother Mark. David learnt the wine trade after spending two years in California at Fresno. He returned to his family's vineyard to join his brother, and in 1976 produced his first commercial vintage, a Cabernet Sauvignon. They employed an army of surfers bumming around on the nearby Margaret River and managed to produce some good wine which they were able to sell successfully.

In 1970, the Hohnens became the third family to plant vines in this now-famous region of Australia

Then inspiration took hold. In 1983, following a technical conference in Perth, some Kiwi winemakers came to visit Margaret River, and left behind some bottles of Penfolds 1983 Sauvignon Blanc. David sampled a glass of this exquisite wine, and made it his mission to find out where in New Zealand the grapes were produced. Although he does not describe himself as a commercially minded person, he was sure there was a market for this fresh, aromatic wine, which was so very different to other wines on the Australian red or Chardonnay-dominated market.

In pursuit of passion

Having experienced what running a winery was like, the family vineyard was now no longer enough for David. After his encounter with the New Zealand Sauvignon Blanc grape, he became passionate about it, and decided to have a go at recreating this wine himself. The following year he attended a wine show in New Zealand and sought out the region where these grapes were produced: Marlborough, near Blenheim at the north of the South Island. His mission: to make a Sauvignon Blanc wine as good as that he had tasted a year previously.

At this wine show he met Kevin Judd, who was then working for Selaks, an established New Zealand winery based in Marlborough. Kevin was to be instrumental in both the conception, and development of David's dream, and would become the first employee of Cloudy Bay, and eventually go on to run it. Kevin was exactly what David needed: experienced in the Marlborough region, and he had worked with Sauvignon for a number of years; the fledgling winery was in safe hands.

Interestingly, David won the prestigious Jimmy Watson trophy two years running, in 1983 and 1984, for his efforts at Cape Mentelle, producing the best one-year red (a red wine that is only one year old) two years running. This stood him in good stead in his new venture, earning him respect and notability in the wine world.

You may have heard the joke about how easy it is to make money from wineries – 'the best way to become a millionaire in the wine business is to start as a multimillionaire and wait for the fortune to dwindle'. As true as it is amusing, this fact makes it very hard to raise capital to start a new winery. In 1985, David approached the financial backers of his Australian venture, with the hope of buying a plot of land in Marlborough. His timing was less than ideal, as Australia's economy was then going through a tough time, and the New Zealand government had just announced they would pay growers NZ$5,000 (which is £5,000 or $8,000 in today's money) an acre to pull up grapevines, as the country had an oversupply problem. Still committed to his vision despite these obstacles, and with help from his brother Mark at Cape Mentelle, David managed to raise A$1m (about £1m or $1.9m today) in debt (albeit at a crazy interest rate of 23%!) and bought a small tract of land in the Marlborough region. He persuaded investors largely due to his reputation in the industry, and his two Jimmy Watson awards – without which, Cloudy Bay may never have materialised.

With this purchase, Cloudy Bay Vineyards was born. David now owned the land and the vines, but there was no winery to process the grapes. So, the young business had to drive 40 tonnes of grapes 400 miles to Corbans winery in Gisborne, where the first batch was pressed. The wine was then tanked and sent to Auckland for bottling. The majority of the first batch was sold in Australia – due to the potential market, and helped along by David's reputation. He was able to use contacts in the wine trade to get the wine on the shelves, and they sold well. Amazingly, the vineyard's first vintage was named the top-rated wine at the 1986 *WINE Magazine* Sauvignon Blanc tasting.

Cloudy Bay delivered a great wine, with a simple, but memorable identity

HOW **THEY** STARTED

Cloudy Bay delivered a great wine, with a simple, but memorable identity. The name Cloudy Bay comes from a local landmark: the Wairau River fills Cloudy Bay with silt, turning it sandy-coloured and cloudy. It was not the first name for the vineyard, however – but David's idea of using another nearby landmark, Farewell Spit, was quickly rejected as not sounding quite right for a wine! Cloudy Bay's distinctively moody label feeds into the Cloudy Bay brand. The label of muted mountains was inspired by a view out overlooking the plane of the Richmond Range.

Growing the product

David regularly commuted from Margaret River, Western Australia to Blenheim, Marlborough. Kevin ran the vineyard day to day, and Cloudy Bay quickly established a pretty comfortable position in the market. The following year, Kevin oversaw the construction of Cloudy Bay's winery and they signed up for 120 tons a year from Corbans. A year on from securing his million-dollar cash, the bank David was with went bust; and he had to refinance in order to finish the winery.

The vineyard itself was run with ease; Kevin tells of music blaring out from huge speakers they had installed in the main cellars, typically Split Enz or Crowded House. And everyone took turns in choosing the playlist.

With the winery now in place, the second vintage was made, and then shipped over to the UK and USA, where once again it received superlative media acclaim. David was already widely respected, due to his success at Cape Mentelle, and ensured his presence was known by hand-delivering bottles to wine writers, complete with a portion of juicy New Zealand green-lip mussels.

David's personal approach worked wonders: British wine connoisseur Hugh Johnson described Cloudy Bay as 'the top name for Sauvignon Blanc' and influential US wine critic Robert Parker agreed: no mean feat when they are famously normally at loggerheads. Wine buffs described it as having 'pungent herbal perfume dancing from the glass, followed by the zing of freshness and light tropical fruits'. In layman's terms: an excellent wine. The beauty of wine distribution is that as soon as you have the critics on board, stockists clamour for your product.

David was already widely respected . . . and ensured his presence was known by hand-delivering bottles to wine writers, complete with a portion of juicy New Zealand green-lip mussels

Cloudy Bay's quick route to the top of the wine charts was explained by Kevin in an interview with *The Telegraph:* 'I think that Cloudy Bay was in the right place at the right time. We found a great site and we have always had a commitment only to produce the finest wines, often at the expense of volume.' Cloudy Bay was able to capitalise on the few vintages that were emerging from New Zealand, and arrived on the scene just as people in Britain and America were turning their heads to the southern hemisphere.

New Zealand wines had already received some international interest, beginning with Montana, which started shipping wine internationally in 1980; Cloudy Bay entered the market at a time of growing interest. Surrounding vineyards, including Montana and Hunters, although already established for five years, could not compete with the quality of Cloudy Bay's product.

Expanding and perfecting

The fledgling winery sought the help of Australian viticulturalist, Richard Smart in 1987, who worked with them, advising on canopy management, which was vital to get the grapes ripe at the right time, with the right flavors. Richard recalls that 'when I arrived, things were well managed, but only on a regional, commercial level.' He was able to hone the product and ensure quality good enough to maintain interest in Cloudy Bay overseas.

Over time, Cloudy Bay developed an effective working team of management, winemakers, viticulturists, and growers. Cloudy Bay gradually acquired more land, and began a relationship with five other vineyards, which contributed to its grape harvest. At the forefront of modern wine technology, Cloudy Bay adopted the Scott Henry Trellis System, which they still use today. This gives a better leaf-to-bunch ratio, ensures more sunlight, and better ripening.

The success of the Sauvignon Blanc was to continue throughout Cloudy Bay's history; but the vineyard began diversifying. In 1987, they introduced their first sparkling wine, Pelorus, and in 1992, the vineyard trialled a barrel-fermented Chardonnay using wild yeasts. This was a great success, and Cloudy Bay introduced Te Koko in 1996. The introduction of Chardonnay and Pinot Noir soon followed. These five wines are produced yearly, with lesser quantities of Riesling and Gewürztraminer also being produced.

The cult of Cloudy Bay

While these new types of wine have met with success, it is Cloudy Bay's signature Sauvignon that keeps the Marlborough vineyard on the map. 60,000 cases of the Sauvignon are produced each year, with the majority sent to the UK and Australia; slightly less goes to the USA – and it all sells out remarkably fast. Just try buying some – it is even rationed by major customers such as The Wine Society in the UK as they simply can't get enough to satisfy demand.

HOW THEY STARTED

60,000 cases of the Sauvignon are produced each year, with the majority sent to the UK and Australia . . . and it all sells out remarkably fast

Indeed, it is fair to say that Cloudy Bay has developed a sort of 'cult' status among wine buffs and consumers alike, especially in the UK. But how did they achieve such interest? Well, it is of course partly to do with the quality of the wine they produce; one wine critic compared drinking Cloudy Bay Vineyard Sauvignon Blanc to hearing Glenn Gould playing Bach's *Goldberg Variations*.

It is also much to do with David Hohnen's keen marketing ability. Whether as a marketing ruse, or simply a question of logistics, a limited batch of Cloudy Bay's yearly vintage is shipped to the UK in October each year, causing prices to rocket and demand to remain unfulfilled. Many retailers double the price of the wine – and it still sells out. British retailers turn to Europe to buy up their quota, pushing the price in the UK up even more.

The business received a massive boost in 1990, when David decided to sell Cloudy Bay (and Cape Mentelle) to Joseph Henriot, then-owner of Veuve Cliquot champagne. This provided a much-needed cash injection which allowed David to take the business to the next level. They expanded markets into Europe and Japan, and continued to roll out a quality product.

Where are they now?

In 2003 luxury goods giant LVMH bought Veuve Cliquot, and with it Cloudy Bay and David's first winery, Cape Mentelle. David has stepped away from the company, and has been replaced by Tony Jordan; Kevin Judd remains with the company. This acquisition has again meant that Cloudy Bay can use the well-established distribution networks of this global company. It is now distributed in 21 European countries, the USA and Canada, Brazil, Asia, Fiji and South Africa. The vineyard has also been expanded recently, with a state-of-the-art new bottling hall. With such a prestigious heavyweight of the champagne and wine world behind them, Cloudy Bay are en route for future expansion – not, we expect, at the expense of its product's quality.

David's new venture has been another vineyard – McHohnen Henry, which he set up with his brother-in-law and is run by his daughter, Freya. He won the inaugural 2007 Len Evans Award for Leadership and is credited with being a fundamental part of bringing New Zealand and Australian wines to the rest of the world.

The Coca-Cola Company

THE COKE SIDE OF BUSINESS

Founders: **John Pemberton (creator) and Asa Griggs Candler (business founder)**

Age of founders at start: **55 and 35**

Background: **Pharmaceuticals and sales**

Year of foundation: **1886**

Business type: **Beverage manufacturer**

Countries now trading in: **Over 200**

Net income and revenue: **£600m ($1.2bn) and £4bn ($7.3bn)**

HOW **THEY** STARTED

veryone has sampled the 'Coke side of life'. Its trademark scripted, bright red logo can be seen all over the world – from English pub umbrellas to football grounds, from Chinese shop signs to 20ft-tall neon advertisements in Times Square, New York. It wouldn't be an exaggeration to say that The Coca-Cola Company is present in every country in the world, and arguably it was the world's first truly global brand. It has been declared both the world's most recognisable trademark and the world's most popular branded drink.

Making a medicine

This amazing success story had very humble beginnings though. A pharmacist named John Pemberton, who lived in Atlanta, Georgia, invented Coca-Cola. One afternoon in 1886, the year when workers were building the Statue of Liberty in New York harbour, he was experimenting with combinations of ingredients in a three-legged brass pot in his backyard to try to develop a new drink. He came up with a fragrant caramel-coloured liquid. Out of sheer curiosity, he took it to neighbouring Jacobs' Pharmacy, where he added carbonated water. After testing it on customers, who all thought this was something special, Jacobs' Pharmacy started selling

JOHN PEMBERTON CONCOCTED THE DRINK IN A BRASS POT IN HIS BACKYARD

it as a medicine for five cents a glass. Pemberton claimed that his new drink cured diseases including morphine addiction, dyspepsia, neurasthenia, headaches, and even impotence.

In the first year, Pemberton sold just nine glasses of Coca-Cola a day, which made him around $50 ($1,140 or £611 today). It had cost Pemberton $70 to create and advertise the drink, so he made a loss. But he persevered; encouraged by the drink's popularity with customers, convinced that he would eventually make something of it.

First named *Pemberton's French Wine of Cola*, the alcohol in the drink was quickly replaced by sugar to make it more appealing to drink. The drink was renamed Coca-Cola by Pemberton's bookkeeper, Frank Robinson, who also wrote the name for the logo in the distinctive script that is still in use today. The name is derived from two key ingredients, taken from leaves from the coca plant, and the caffeine-rich kola nut. Until 1905, the drink even contained traces of cocaine, there for its medicinal effects.

> The name Coca-Cola is derived from two key ingredients, taken from leaves from the coca plant, and the caffeine-rich kola nut

Pemberton's young company started to grow sales of its drink by getting other pharmacies to sell Coca-Cola too. It sold 25 gallons of syrup to drugstores, and ensured all the stores that sold the drink had hand-painted Coca-Cola signs to help promote it. Pemberton persuaded six local businessmen to invest in the company to help him finance this expansion.

Coca-Cola's famous advertising campaigns have their roots right at the beginning of its history: soon after the drink had been created, Pemberton placed the first newspaper advert in *The Atlanta Journal*, inviting people to try 'the new and popular soda fountain drink'.

Sadly, Pemberton died in 1888, and so never saw his drink taken to the masses. The person to do this was Atlantan businessman Asa Griggs Candler, who bought the rights to the drink for $2,300 ($52,400 or £28,000 today). It took Candler three years to secure rights to the business, as a very ill Pemberton had also sold rights to another businessman, and given exclusive rights to his son, which took some time to unravel.

Candler had a vision for the brand, to turn the now-popular drink from a beverage into a business. He disbanded the pharmaceutical arm of the company and partnered with his brother, John Candler and Pemberton's bookkeeper Frank Robinson. Together they raised $100,000 ($2,280 or £1,298 today), then a very substantial sum, to kick-start the business.

In 1891, Candler had full control of the business, and within a year, he had increased the sale of Coca-Cola syrup tenfold. In 1892 the company was incorporated, and The Coca-Cola Company was officially born.

HOW **THEY STARTED**

They began a huge marketing campaign, using new advertising techniques. To spread the word, he gave away coupons for free Coca-Cola tasters in newspapers, and offered pharmacists two gallons of the syrup, if they would agree to give away one gallon's worth as free samples when people produced his coupon. He supplied the pharmacists with urns, clocks, calendars and scales all bearing the brand name. The combination of this strongly branded approach and a drink which almost everyone loved, worked wonders, and sales grew fast. By 1895, just four years later, Candler had grown demand enough that he needed to build syrup plants in Chicago, Dallas and Los Angeles, and declared to his shareholders that 'Coca-Cola is now consumed in every state and territory in the United States'. Today it is sufficiently easy to launch a product nationally that it is easy to miss just what a major achievement this is. This was an era when it took days to travel across the country, when there was no radio or television, and so to be available in every state so quickly is quite phenomenal.

Up until 1894, Coca-Cola was only sold by the glassful, until a Mississippi businessman named Joseph Biedenharn bottled Coca-Cola at his factory and sent a dozen to Candler. Candler hated the product and quickly dismissed it. He overlooked this crucial development again in 1899, when two lawyers from Chattanooga, Tennessee, Benjamin F Thomas and Joseph B Whitehead secured exclusive rights from Candler to bottle and sell the beverage in nearly all of the USA – for only one dollar. In fact Candler was so sure that this idea wouldn't amount to anything that he didn't even bother collecting the dollar!

This was the start of the unusual corporate structure which continues to this day. The Coca-Cola Company supplies syrup, called concentrate, to customers all over the world. Some of these customers are restaurants and bars which sell the drink by the glass, like the original pharmacy retailers, while the other group of customers are bottling companies, who add carbonated water to the syrup in a factory, and bottle it for sale in shops.

1899-1902   1900-1916   1915   1957   1961   1991   1994

COCA-COLA'S BOTTLE PROGRESSION OVER NEARLY A CENTURY

Thomas and Whitehead began by opening bottling plants in Chattanooga and Atlanta, but soon realised that there was a better way for them to roll out bottled Coca-Cola across the country. The two Chattanooga lawyers were joined by another, and the trio split the USA into three territories, and began selling the bottling rights to local entrepreneurs; not only did this reduce the amount of capital the lawyers needed, as each local entrepreneur used his own money, but it also provided local knowledge and the commitment of business owners which would have been very hard to set up any other way. The first sub-licensed bottler began in 1900, and by 1909, there were 400 Coca-Cola bottling plants in the country.

By the turn of the century, Candler had increased Coca-Cola's sales to 40 times their 1890 level, and his continuing advertising campaign and his free samples had spread the name 'Coca-Cola' across America.

Bubbling overseas

The drink was first taken overseas by Candler's son Charles. On a trip to London, Charles took a jug of syrup with him, and totted up modest orders for five gallons. Coca-Cola was first sold in England on 31 August 1900, and gradually built enough momentum to be sold in Selfridges and The London Coliseum.

After seeing the success of the bottled drinks in the USA, The Coca-Cola Company decided to licence out bottling rights to overseas territories itself. The first international bottling plants began in 1906 in Canada, Cuba and Panama, with others, including the Philippines and Guam following shortly afterwards in 1912 and 1917 respectively. As he had done so effectively in the USA, Candler supported the new supplies of drinks with a thorough marketing campaign, to ensure the bright red logo was seen in shops and cafés everywhere.

Candler supported the new supplies of drinks with a thorough marketing campaign, to ensure the bright red logo was seen in shops and cafés everywhere

Most of the companies granted the rights to bottle Coca-Cola in different countries were brewers. This worked well, as the brewers already had bottling plants and expertise, so it was relatively easy and quick for them to add the new drink to their range. The brewers also already had distribution through their own existing customer base, which meant that Coca-Cola got access to shops, bars and restaurants far faster than it would have done had it set up a brand-new business from scratch in a new country.

The drink had become very well known, and was clearly successful, so inevitably a number of competitors appeared, though of course none knew the precise recipe for the drink, which was kept utterly secret. The Coca-Cola Company started to get concerned that it was too easy for customers to be given a different drink and mistakenly think that it was 'The Real Thing', which not only meant that Coca-Cola lost out on the sale, but also potentially that customers would not enjoy the rival drink as much and might not buy Coca-Cola the next time. Something needed to be done. So the company decided to come up with a distinctive bottle to ensure their product stood out. It was in 1916, following a design contest, that the now-famous bottle was first used, designed by the Root Glass Company of Terre Haute, Indiana. The winning design was chosen for its attractive appearance, original design, and because, even in the dark, people could easily identify it as the genuine article.

New leadership, new vision

After nearly three decades of turning the drink into a substantial and successful business, Candler eventually sold the business in 1919 to Ernest Woodruff for $25m (worth roughly $341m or £183m in today's money); his son Robert became president in 1923. The company was reincorporated as a Delaware corporation and listed on the New York stock exchange, selling 500,000 shares to the general public for $40 per share. Coca-Cola was now firmly established in the USA; Woodruff's mission was to go global, and his vision: to create a brand that was 'in arm's reach of desire'.

During the 1920s and 1930s Woodruff set his sights on international expansion. By the time Woodruff took over in 1923, Coca-Cola was strongly established in North America, had some bottling arrangements in South America, and had just opened its first European bottling plant in France. From this base, Woodruff's Coca-Cola went on in the 1920s to open plants in Guatemala, Honduras, Mexico, Belgium and Italy. In 1926, Coca-Cola set up a Foreign Department, which became the Coca-Cola Export Corporation in 1930. In all countries where Coca-Cola had sprung up, a creative, vibrant and culturally relevant advertising campaign followed.

A significant international move occurred in 1928, when Woodruff began the partnership with the Olympic games in Amsterdam. A thousand bottles of Coca-Cola accompanied the US team, and the drink was on sale in the Olympic stadium. Vendors were adorned with caps and coats emblazoned with the Coca-Cola logo, and the drink was also sold at surrounding cafés, restaurants and shops. Elsewhere, Woodruff had the company logo decorating racing dog sleds in Canada, and around the bullfighting arenas of Spain. By the start of the Second World War, Coca-Cola was present in 44 countries. A marketing genius, Woodruff developed the company's successful, but limited line, introducing the six-pack (making the drinks more transportable and encouraging people to buy in bulk) and the open-top cooler. Coca-Cola was available in vending machines from 1929 and was advertised on the radio from 1930. In 1935, bottlers hired women to act as door-to-door salespeople for the drink, with a target of 125 calls per day.

In a marketing scheme that was to have repercussions for little children everywhere, during Christmas 1931, Coca-Cola's famous red Santa Claus made its debut, banishing the long-established and previously unchallenged green Santa into the mists of time.

Coke's wartime effort

Throughout the Second World War, Coca-Cola continued to manufacture, even offering the drink for five cents to any serviceperson, whatever country they were in, no matter the cost to the company. Bottling plants were opened to supply troops with the drink, following a request from General Eisenhower himself on 29 June 1943, requesting the shipment of materials for 10 bottling plants to be sent to North Africa along with three million bottles of Coca-Cola and enough supplies to make the same amount twice a month. Coca-Cola responded within six months, and set up a bottling plant in Algiers.

SANTA CLAUS DRESSED IN RED IS NOW A GLOBALLY RECOGNISED FIGURE

In all, 64 bottling plants opened during the war, and more than five billion bottles of Coca-Cola were consumed by service people. Mobile service stations were also taken to the battlefields, and people throughout Europe and the Pacific had their first taste of the drink. These wartime bottling plants were later converted and run by local civilians, who continued to produce and sell the drink even after the Americans had left.

Promoting global happiness

Post-war America was the perfect place for Coca-Cola to expand – people were embracing a carefree lifestyle, and Coca-Cola's advertising mirrored this desire, with images of loved-up couples at the drive-in, and happy families driving round in shiny cars. Coca-Cola continued to be served at soda fountains, and was added to the menu in ice cream parlours.

By now the company still had just one product, albeit an extraordinarily successful one, and it began experimenting with new flavours. It introduced Fanta in the 1950s (which was originally concocted in wartime Germany), followed by Sprite in 1961, TAB in 1963 and Fresca in 1966. The company acquired the Minute Maid Company in 1960, branching out into juices. New lines of Coca-Cola were also rolled out, including bigger bottles and metal cans in 1960.

The 1950s and 1960s saw bottling plants built in more countries, including Cambodia, Montserrat, Paraguay, Macau and Turkey. During the global economic boom of the 1970s and 1980s, many of Coca-Cola's small and medium-sized bottlers joined forces to better serve their growing international customer base. By 1969, for the first time, Coca-Cola sales in international markets exceeded those in the USA.

In 1971 Coca-Cola created a particularly special television advertisement, that saw young people from all over the world gather on an hilltop in Italy to sing 'I'd Like to Buy the World a Coke'. Coca-Cola had made its mark on the international market, and for a time, was seen as an icon of unity, in an era that had not yet grasped the consequences of globalisation. Significantly, in 1978, the People's Republic of China declared The Coca-Cola Company as the only company allowed to sell packaged cold drinks in China.

Coca-Cola had made its mark on the international market, and for a time, was seen as an icon of unity, in an era that had not yet grasped the consequences of globalisation

Intelligent risk taking

In 1981, Roberto C Goizueta became chairman of the board of directors and CEO of The Coca-Cola Company, and decided to take the company forward with a strategy he called 'intelligent risk taking'. This began with the introduction of Diet Coke on Independence Day 1982, the very first extension of the Coca-Cola trademark. Coke's arch rival Pepsi had released their diet version of the drink in 1963, with great success. Despite its comparatively late entry, within two years Diet Coke had become the top low-calorie drink in the world. Coke might have been slow on the uptake, but quickly followed Diet Coke's inception with a range of alternatives, including caffeine-free Coke and Cherry Coke.

Goizueta's riskiest initiative began in 1985, when he released a new-tasting Coca-Cola, the first change in formula for 99 years. Why fix something that isn't broken? Well, it was breaking: Coke's share of the soft drinks market had decreased from 60% at the end of the Second World War, to less than 24% in 1983, in large part due to its new rival, Pepsi. Its share price had also decreased by 2.5% in the last four years (that might sound like a small percentage, but represented a drop in market capitalisation of $500m (£400m). Pepsi had directly challenged Coke's success in the marketplace by conducting blind taste testing on the streets of America, with many people opting for the sweeter Pepsi. This saw Pepsi overtake Coke in supermarket sales.

'New Coke' passed taste testers' approval in extensive testing before launch, being preferred to Pepsi by most, but didn't succeed in the marketplace. In an unprecedented expression of brand loyalty, people demanded their old Coke back. Coca-Cola received over 40,000 pleading letters and their phone lines were continually blocked with customers desperate to have their old drink back again. The company's market share fell to as low as 1.4%. Critics named the initiative the biggest marketing blunder ever, and Pepsi declared themselves the victor of the 'cola wars'. The company listened, and after 79 days of New Coke, they started supplying the original Coca-Cola again, labelled Coca-Cola Classic, selling alongside its younger relation.

Its return was momentous: ABC News' Peter Jennings interrupted regular programming to share the news with viewers, and speaking to the senate, US senator David Pryor called the reintroduction 'a meaningful moment in US history'. More importantly, its sales leapt up, reclaiming top spot, which it has never lost since. New Coke was slowly discontinued, and the original recipe is still used today.

They started supplying the original Coca-Cola again, labelled Coca-Cola Classic . . . sales leapt up, reclaiming top spot, which it has never lost since

HOW **THEY** STARTED

In an effort to help manage the now-substantial network of bottlers, the company set up Coca-Cola Enterprises Inc in 1986. This new public company was intended to organise the bottling partners, and ensure they could meet the international demand for Coke. The company follows the same approach today: Coca-Cola work with local bottlers, some of whom are public companies, some are independent and family-owned; significantly the majority of them are not owned by Coca-Cola. The bottling plants (of which there are now 300) package, distribute and market the product.

In 1985, Coca-Cola became the first independent operator in the Soviet Union, and throughout the early 1990s, invested heavily in building bottling plants in eastern Europe.

Flying high

During the 1990s, Coke made its presence known in the sporting world, sponsoring the Olympic games, FIFA World Cup, Rugby World Cup and the National Basketball Association. 1993 saw the introduction of the incredibly catchy 'Always Coca-Cola' advertising campaign, and by 1997, the company was selling one billion servings of its products every day.

One of the last countries to have the pleasure of Coca-Cola's presence was India: as Indian law forbade companies to trade if they withheld trade-secret information, something Coca-Cola insisted upon to protect their formula. In 1993, India changed its laws regarding trademarks, and Coca-Cola went on sale. A populous and hot country, India seemed fertile ground for the international giant, but surprisingly struggled to capture the market. Its

COCA-COLA CLASSIC WAS BROUGHT BACK DUE TO PUBLIC DEMAND

slow growth was aided by the acquisition of Indian brands Limca, Maaza and Thums Up. The company followed this pattern of growth by acquisition in other countries too, and acquired Barq's root beer in the USA and Inca Kola in Peru.

In 1999 The Coca-Cola Company purchased the soft drinks brands of Cadbury Schweppes plc in various countries, including Great Britain. This expanded the existing product range of beverages such as Coca-Cola, Diet Coke, Cherry Coca-Cola, Fanta, Sprite, Lilt and Five Alive to include the Schweppes' range of drinks such as Dr Pepper, Oasis, Kia-Ora and Malvern water.

Where are they now?

The Coca-Cola Company now owns more than 400 brands and sells more than 1.5 billion beverage servings each day. Over its lifespan, it has produced more than 10 billion gallons of syrup. Out of all countries Coca-Cola dominates, the highest per capita consumption are in Mexico and Iceland. The company employs over 90,000 people and is headed up by Muhtar Kent, president and CEO. To celebrate its heritage, The New World of Coca-Cola opened in 2007, an attraction dedicated to the brand, and is now one of Atlanta's main tourist attractions.

Now a major global corporation already mature in many of its markets, Coca-Cola faces new challenges, from changing patterns of demand for soft drinks in many developed

A RANGE OF INTERNATIONAL BOTTLES: COCA–COLA WAS THE FIRST GLOBALLY RECOGNISED BRAND

HOW **THEY STARTED**

THE COMPANY IS CONSULTANTLY INNOVATING ITS PRODUCTS AND HAS
RECENTLY LAUNCH DIET COKE WITH ADDED VITAMINS AND MINERALS

countries to enormous and fast-growing potential in the increasingly affluent countries
such as China. Coca-Cola continues to add to its extensive brand list, including the launch
of Coke Zero in 2005, and other acquisitions including water and tea companies. Recently,
Coca-Cola has launched its first ever clothing range, sustainable apparel. Sold in
Wal-Mart, the t-shirts are made of recycled plastic Coke bottles.

Today, 72% of Coca-Cola is sold outside the USA, and Coca-Cola's share price continues
to rise, based on expectations of continued profitable growth to come.

GREEN &BLACK'S

ORGANIC

Green & Black's

SWEET LIKE CHOCOLATE

Founders: **Craig Sams and Josephine Fairley**

Age of founders at start: **47 and 35**

Background: **Restaurateur and journalist**

Year of foundation: **1991**

Business type: **Chocolate maker**

Countries now trading in: **Over 20 countries worldwide**

Turnover: **£40m ($70m)**

HOW **THEY** STARTED

G reen & Black's is the fastest growing chocolate confectionary brand in the world. Established in 1991 to support the Mayan Indians of Belize it now sells over £40m ($70m)of chocolate products a year has around 40 employees and has operations in the USA, Australia and South-East Asia.

Its story is a heady mix of innovation, ethics, business and fair trade; in short, a great example of how to successfully launch the right product at the right time with extraordinary amounts of self belief and passion in what you're doing.

Of late it has branched out into ice cream, cereal bars, biscuits and chocolate-flavoured drinks. The company uses organically sourced cocoa beans, from Belize and the Dominican Republic; it is estimated that Green & Black's uses a third of the world's organic cocoa.

Snapped up by confectionary giant Cadbury Schweppes in 2005 for an estimated £20m ($36m) (they'd bought an initial 5% stake in 2003), the brand is worth around £40m ($75m) and remains a stand-alone business within the Cadbury's empire. Green & Black's have totally dominated the organic chocolate market – they have an estimated 90% almighty chunk. From an original stall at the Portobello Market in 1991, Green & Black's products are available at most major food retailers, such as Britain's Waitrose, Sainsbury's and Tesco as well as various ethical shopping websites. Whilst its head office is based in London, the chocolate is made by a family-owned business in Italy's Lake Como region.

CRAIG SANS AND JOSEPHINE FAIRLEY HAVE BROUGHT THE WORLD ORGANIC CHOCOLATE

One bite changes everything

Founders and husband and wife team Craig Sams and Josephine Fairley were no strangers to the ethical food market. Craig had a history of hippy chic – he'd founded Ceres, Britain's first organic bakery, on Portobello Road in 1972 and also opened Britain's first macrobiotic restaurant in Notting Hill in 1967 (way before anyone would associate the term with Madonna and Gwyneth).

A bold innovator, Craig introduced brown rice and tamari (wheat-free soy sauce) into the UK, and he was behind the revolutionary method of using apple juice instead of sugar to sweeten jam. He also created the Whole Earth brand which launched the world's first whole-nut peanut butter and he is also chairman of the Soil Association, the British charity dedicated to sustainable organic farming and human health.

Josephine, originally inspired to 'go green' by a copy of *The Shopper's Guide to Saving the Planet* in 1971, was the environmental correspondent for *The Times* newspaper and had also written its column on organic living.

So if anyone was going to provide the world with an exciting, ethical and truly innovative chocolate range, it was these two. Real environmental crusaders, ahead of their time and passionate about chocolate, they wanted to leave some sort of ethical legacy.

The pivotal moment was a simple one. Josephine happened to taste a half-eaten bar of dark 70% chocolate left on Craig's desk. Made from organic cocoa beans, it had been sent to Craig as a sample. It was love at first bite for Josephine and the couple embarked on a voyage of discovery to create the world's first organic chocolate bar.

Josephine describes this epiphany in the founders' book, *Sweet Dreams, The Story of Green & Black's* (Random House 2008), 'As this square of dark chocolate melted on my tongue, I knew my hunt for chocolate heaven was over.'

Real environmental crusaders, ahead of their time and passionate about chocolate, they wanted to leave some sort of ethical legacy

Getting off the ground

The sales and distribution infrastructure was already there, courtesy of the Whole Foods business in Portobello. With her journalistic experience, Josephine knew an organic, 70% cocoa solids bar, was 'news'; she was put in charge of marketing, and stumping up the £20,000 ($34,000) cash injection to kick-start the business, a responsibility which terrified her.

HOW **THEY** STARTED

When it came to settling on a name, they wanted something classy, imparting a sense of confectionary history. With a respectful nod to the crème de la crème of chocolate brands (such as Charbonnel & Walker and Callard & Bowser), they decided their name had to have an 'Et' (ampersand) in the middle. 'Green' would represent their ethical stance and 'Black' the dark, almost 'blackness' of the 70% cocoa solids in their first historic bar of chocolate. And thus Green & Black's was born. Craig and Josephine believe the inclusion of the ampersand somehow made them seem more like an established company, like they had been around for years. Little did they know that forever more, they'd be fielding curious questions about the true identity of 'Mr Green' and 'Mr Black'.

> *'Green' would represent their ethical stance and 'Black' the dark, almost 'blackness' of the 70% cocoa solids in their first historic bar of chocolate*

Their timing was just right. Retailers were excited by an opportunity to throw off outdated and clichéd notions of healthy food and stock the world's first organic chocolate. Craig admits that the real challenge was getting chocolate consumers into a new way of thinking – and buying Green & Black's. A reporter, chocolate lover and a woman, Josephine hit the nail on the head perfectly with her first PR pitch – lauding Green & Black's as 'almost' guilt-free chocolate. The launch was a huge success.

Thanks to a recommendation from Lady Sainsbury herself following a dinner party sampling, Sainsbury's was the first supermarket to stock Green & Black's, soon followed by Safeway. Word of mouth was key in spreading their message and taste. With no marketing budget to speak of, they 'piggy-backed' on their Whole Foods business, setting up stalls at trade fairs in London, Germany and the USA. It was slow work, but it paid off, as the company built up interests in overseas markets including Denmark, Finland, Sweden, Australia, New Zealand and the USA.

Although costly, and tiring, these trade shows proved worthwhile, as the founders describe in *Sweet Dreams*, 'you get to peek at what the competition is up to. You get to make those contacts . . . it was hugely heartening to get feedback that our chocolate potentially had a market beyond the UK's borders'.

Spicing it up

Inspired by a trip to Belize in 1994, Craig and Josephine decided to research mixing their chocolate with spices and citrus; to their delight, the resulting concoction was similar to the traditional Mayan drink 'kukuh', drunk during ceremonial dances.

Exclusively stocked by Sainsbury's for the first six months, 'Maya Gold' was made with cocoa sourced from cooperative producers in Belize, Central America. The original 100mg Maya Gold bar was the first product in the UK to be awarded the Fairtrade mark in 1994. It was another fantastic story with which to promote their product and raise awareness of their organic ethos. Maya Gold had taken just under a year to go from original concept to national distribution and global awareness.

> *The original 100mg Maya Gold bar was the first product in the UK to be awarded the Fairtrade mark in 1994*

Buoyed by their success and burgeoned by their passion for delivering real flavour, by the late 1990s they developed more bars in the Green & Black's series: milk, hazelnut and currant, mint and white. They discovered the best weather for sales (dry) and the worst (snow and heat waves) and while cautious about overextending their brand, decided that branching into ice cream was right for them.

They've won several awards along the way, including the Worldaware Award Organic Food Awards (won in 1993, 1995 and 1996) and the Good Housekeeping Award in 2008 for Favourite Comfort Food. They were also the first winners of the 1992 Ethical Consumer Association's Ethical Product award.

GREEN & BLACK'S MILK CHOCOLATE WAS INTRODUCED IN THE LATE 1990s

HOW **THEY** STARTED

Investment injection

In 1996, William Kendall, the entrepreneur behind the New Covent Garden Soup brand, together with 11 backers including business partner Nick Beart, acquired an 80% stake in Green & Black's. At that time, the chocolate maker was making a loss although it was turning over £2m ($3m). The investors insisted that the founders retained less than 30% in the business, so they couldn't exercise any difficult rights under UK company law, so Sams and Fairley sold 80% of their shares for £4m ($6m) and kept a 20% stake in the business. While the ownership change was a difficult one to come to terms with for the founders (Craig and Josephine describe it as 'vendor remorse') they were also convinced it was right for the business: 'we felt our baby was in good hands and there was money and talent to drive it forward.' With Kendall at the helm the business continued to grow strongly, with turnover reaching £22.4m ($40m) in the year to February 2005.

Kendall wanted to transform the business from a niche company for the ethically literate to a more global, money-making operation. While he agreed with the values of Green & Black's, he believed that running it at a loss would negate the very point of the business: helping the Mayan farmers.

Craig was made president, a new PR firm was brought in and as CEO Kendall took a firm hold of marketing. Josephine, however, found the transition difficult as her main roles were transferred elsewhere. Ultimately, with Craig's guidance, and the advice that she could either have the money or the control, but not both, she stopped worrying.

THE COCOA BEANS ARE SOURCED FROM BELIZE AND THE DOMINICAN REPUBLIC

Despite bearing the popular tag of 'ethical business', Kendall takes quite a hard-nosed approach to the business, believing quality rather than conscience will ensure their long-term future. In an interview with the *Financial Times* in 2004, he explained, 'You have to build a business around a really good product. You cannot build your business around being ethical because there is someone who can come out and be more ethical than you'.

Where are they now?

After the Cadbury deal in 2005, Kendall faced accusations of selling out and putting at risk the livelihoods of the communities in Belize's jungles which harvest the cocoa. But he says he did it for the shareholders – it's his job to ensure them a good return on their investment. And with the global weight of the Cadbury Schweppes empire behind them, Green & Black's can give the US market a run for its money; it's already outselling luxury chocolatiers such as Lindt in some British markets so the sector can expect them to pack a mighty punch.

Cadbury insist they remain committed to ethical business. And who wouldn't, considering the difference it's making to the bottom line and their global image? Interestingly, the founders of Cadbury were ardent Quakers and consequently passionate advocates of social equality; perhaps the match is a good one.

But how do the founders feel about the Cadburys takeover? Josephine comments that 'If you had asked me on day one who I'd have liked to sell the company to, I would have said Cadbury's . . . We were lucky to find such great buyers because quite often, sadly, all venture capitalists or investors are interested in is maximum return, not a sale that comes with a feel-good factor by way of a bonus'.

Craig and Josephine now run their new organic venture, Judges Bakery, in Hastings. As well as offering the full range of Green & Black's, the bakery also won top prize for Best New Store in the Natural Products Awards. Craig has recently retired from being the chairman of the Soil Association and is president of Green & Black's. Cadbury has given them an unprecedented opportunity to expand their brand to a whole new level – it will be exciting to see what chocolate concoction they come up with next.

KFC

THE RECIPE FOR SUCCESS

Founder: **Harland Sanders**

Age of founder at start: **56**

Background: **Farm hand, railroad operator, justice of peace, insurance salesman**

Year of foundation: **1952**

Business type: **Fast-food chicken restaurant and takeaway**

Countries now trading in: **More than 100**

Turnover: **$520.3m (£260m) (2007)**

HOW **THEY** STARTED

When Harland Sanders opened a small roadside restaurant in the USA in the 1930s specialising in fried chicken, he could not have predicted the legacy he would create. That one site based in Louisville, Kentucky has today grown into Kentucky Fried Chicken (more recently renamed KFC), a business with 14,800 company-owned and franchised restaurants in more than 100 countries. The business has expanded from its humble origins into a global superbrand and is now as famous for its chicken as it is for its strapline – 'finger-lickin' good' – and the snow-white bearded image of its founder, known more commonly as Colonel Sanders.

Home is where the business is

Harland was born in Indiana in 1890 with a taste for fried chicken honed from an early age. He enjoyed cooking the food his mother had taught him to make, including pan-fried chicken, country ham, fresh vegetables and homemade biscuits.

But it was some time before he could put these home-grown skills to use. Harland left school at the tender age of 12 and proved his entrepreneurial credentials by trying all manner of jobs – including stints as a farm hand, railroading, selling insurance and even serving as a justice of the peace. He also gained experience starting two companies – one was a steamboat ferry company that operated on the Ohio River between Jeffersonville and Louisville and the other a manufacturing business.

His real love, however, came from doing what he knew best – cooking. In 1930, despite the fact that the USA was in the grip of the Depression, he opened his first restaurant in the front room of a petrol station he had acquired in Corbin, Kentucky. It was a modest setting, consisting of one table and six chairs. The idea had come from conversations with his customers. Harland had spotted the opportunity to serve food after customers who had stopped for petrol asked if they could get food nearby. He named the site Sanders Court & Café and his entrepreneurial skills were put to good use as he juggled several roles, including station operator, chief cook and cashier.

Harland had spotted the opportunity to serve food after customers who had stopped for petrol asked if they could get food nearby

Word soon spread about his cuisine, so much so that in 1936, Kentucky Governor Ruby Laffoon made Harland an honorary Kentucky Colonel in recognition of his contributions to the state's cuisine. Customers were soon turning up in droves for the food alone, which prompted Harland to expand to bigger premises across the street, a building that housed a 142-seat restaurant as well as a motel and a petrol station. He enrolled on an eight-week course in restaurant and hotel management at Cornell University to learn more about the business and forged ambitious plans to start a restaurant chain by expanding with two further sites. Both of the new sites, however, failed soon after they started, so he concentrated on improving the existing business.

Spice of life

Some might say that Harland was a late bloomer – it wasn't until 1940, when he was 50 years old, that he created the recipe that the business is so famous for today. But as he said in his autobiography, *Life as I have known it has been finger lickin' good* (Creation House 1974), 'no hours, nor amount of labour, nor amount of money would deter me from giving the best that was in me.'

Fried chicken, too, might not have been a new concept, but Harland proved that not all successful ideas need to be new by coming up with his own original recipe of different herbs and seasoning. It gave a new twist to one of the nation's favourite foods. He claimed that the 11 herbs and spices he used 'stand on everybody's shelf', ensuring the chicken had that home-cooked feel about it. 'I hand-mixed the spices in those days like mixing cement,' he once said, 'on a specially cleaned concrete floor on my back porch in Corbin.'

He claimed that the 11 herbs and spices he used 'stand on everybody's shelf', ensuring the chicken had that home-cooked feel about it

Not satisfied with perfecting the herbs and spices for fried chicken, Harland decided to experiment with the way it was cooked. He braved the pressure cooker, a new invention at the time, in his quest for the perfect fried chicken. He developed a method of pressure-frying the chicken so it could be cooked much faster than using traditional frying methods in an iron skillet – cutting the cooking time by more than a third. Again, this was in response to his customers' needs – they weren't prepared to wait a long time for their food. Testament to his success thus far was the fact that the motel and restaurant was endorsed by food critic Duncan Hines in *Adventures in Good Eating* in 1939, a guide to America's finest roadside restaurants. The listing sent the restaurant's popularity soaring.

Testing times

In the years that followed, though, a series of events that were out of Harland's hands forced him to radically alter his original business plan. In 1939, a fire destroyed the original building, but Harland rebuilt and reopened the restaurant. The advent of the Second World War, however, posed an even bigger challenge – a ration on petrol forced Harland to close the motel. Undaunted, he reopened after the war, and business boomed for many years, as his restaurant and motel was a popular stop for travellers driving along what was then the major north-south route.

Harland even became an early pioneer of the franchising model – he travelled from town to town cooking batches of his fried chicken for other restaurant owners and employees. Sales were slow but his dogged perseverance paid off and resulted in his first franchise operation in 1952, when Harland gave Pete Harman of Salt Lake City the first Kentucky Fried Chicken franchise. The deal was done the old-fashioned way – a handshake agreement stipulated a payment of five cents (about $0.40 or £0.21 today) to Harland for each chicken sold.

> *Harland even became an early pioneer of the franchising model – he travelled from town to town cooking batches of his fried chicken for other restaurant owners and employees*

Not all progress had a happy ending, however. Transport development plans in the late 1950s were to prove too big a hurdle for even Harland to overcome and put paid to his business – in more ways than one. The completion of an interstate highway provided travellers with an alternative north-south route, one which completely bypassed the restaurant. The value of Harland's site plummeted as customer numbers dwindled and he was forced to sell the business and try his luck elsewhere. The sale – for $75,000 ($58,000 or £31,000 today), half the asking price of the previous year – was completed on the day he officially 'retired' and picked up his first social security cheque for $105.

After paying off debts, he was virtually penniless, but ever the entrepreneur – even in his 60s – and armed with a strong belief in his fried chicken product, Harland adapted his business plan. If customers weren't able to come to his restaurant and try his recipes, he would have to take the idea to them. It was at this point that plans for a KFC franchise gathered momentum.

The road to success

With the first franchise in Salt Lake City going well, Harland went on the road to sell his recipe to restaurants, but he had to go right back to basics. 'Lots of nights I would sleep in the back of my car so I would have enough money to buy cookers the next day if someone took a franchise,' he recalled in his autobiography.

It was also a case of all hands on deck – Harland's wife, as he put it, acted as 'my packing girl, my warehouse supervisor, my delivery person – you name it. Our garage was the warehouse. She'd fill the day's orders in little paper sacks with cellophane linings and package them for shipment. Then she had to put them on a midnight train.'

Harland came up with a package he would sell to restaurants: the recipe (which included the spices), a pressure cooker, carryout cartons and advertising material. He also persuaded existing restaurant owners to add the KFC formula to their menus.

The hard work paid off and the concept known as Kentucky Fried Chicken took shape, and quickly became a fast food sensation. By 1963, the recipe was franchised to more than 600 outlets in the USA and Canada. Harland visited independent restaurants throughout the USA, doing a spot of what he called 'Coloneling' – ensuring that customers were happy. It marked a turning-point in the business in more ways than one.

Expansion wasn't Harland's sole growth strategy and he constantly sought to innovate the business. The first takeaway was offered at a restaurant in Jacksonville, Florida, in 1957 inspired by an idea from Harland's daughter Margaret. Also in 1957, the chicken was sold in containers they called buckets, along with the slogan, 'finger lickin' good'. For the first time and by 1960, Harland's vision of bringing the recipe to the people had well and truly paid off, with 190 franchisees running 400 franchise sites across the USA and Canada.

Going global

Three years on, in 1963, the business was thriving with 17 employees, but it was getting too big for Harland to handle. In the last year alone, he had travelled 200,000 miles to drum up new business and cater for existing franchisees and he was not getting any younger. An attractive offer from an investment group headed by John Brown, Jack Massey and Pete Harman (the first person to buy into the franchise 12 years ago) proved hard to refuse. Harland agreed to sell for the then substantial sum of $2m, ($14m or £7.5m today) on condition that he still kept a hand in the business, as an ambassador for the company. He was in charge of quality control and his image was used as the company trademark. Under the terms of the agreement, the investment group bought national and international franchise rights, excluding England, Florida, Utah and Montana. Harland also retained ownership of the franchises in Canada

The new owners pumped investment funds into the business and the company set its next sights on expanding more, both within North America and globally. Soon KFC outlets spanned 50 states in the USA and the business was established in Puerto Rico, Mexico, Japan, Jamaica and the Bahamas. The first European site opened in Preston, England, in 1964. In the mid-1960s, Kentucky Fried Chicken ranked sixth in volume among food-service companies, with 1,500 takeaways and restaurants. Franchising remained the core of the business' expansion plans and the now well-known red and white striped buildings were developed to attract tourists and residents to the brand.

> *Franchising remained the core of the business' expansion plans and the now well-known red and white striped buildings were developed to attract tourists and residents to the brand*

In 1966 the Kentucky Fried Chicken Advertising Co-op was established, giving franchisees 10 votes and the company three when deciding advertising budgets and campaigns. Franchisees also benefited from a cut of company equipment and supply sales and a National Franchisee Advisory Council had also been established.

Buoyed with the success of the business' rapid expansion, the company went public, listing on the New York Stock Exchange in 1969, with Harland buying the first 100 shares.

At this point the new owners were looking at ways to streamline the business. Plans to reduce overheads, in particular labour costs, were put into action, by transforming Harland's original idea of a sit-down eatery into a fast-food, stand-up concept, with emphasis on fast service. The business grew at a phenomenal rate, and some franchisees had already become millionaires. But Kentucky Fried Chicken found that such growth was to come at a price. With franchisees making money at such a fast rate, there was very little incentive for them to stay with KFC in the long term instead of turning to new ventures (at one point the management team had 21 millionaires reporting to it!). This meant that successful franchisees were only prepared to commit to the business for a year or two, contributing to a lack of strongly established, and experienced, franchisees.

At the same time, negative reports about the accounting practices of other franchise operations appeared in the media and as a result, although not connected to KFC, the company's share price took a battering, dropping to $10 per share after a high of $55.50 a year before. It signalled a worrying time for the business and several key players, including Jack Massey, resigned from the business following a series of disagreements. A new management team, with a background in food and finance, was swiftly appointed to revive financial fortunes. It signalled the end of the road for Harland's involvement with the company and he resigned from the board of directors. At the grand old age of 80, even he knew his limits. In an article in the *New York Times*, he says: '[I] realised that I was someplace I had no place being ... Everything that a board of a big corporation does is over my head and I'm confused by the talk and high finance discussed at these meetings.'

Changing hands

As part of the plan to revive Kentucky Fried Chicken, the business merged with food and alcoholic beverage business Heublein Inc in 1971, when sales stood at $700m (£280m), and John Brown left the business following this deal. It seemed a wise move as Heublein's expertise was in marketing, an area in which the business received a much-needed boost. Introducing new product ranges, such as barbecued ribs, was also the order of the day and although the new lines proved popular, in reality, they masked the fact that sales of fried chicken were in decline. The benefit of this began to wane after a while, though, and the business once again began to falter.

By the early 1970s, relationships with existing franchisees in the USA were also at an all-time low, a problem that had been brewing since Brown and Massey had bought the business. Franchisees were at this time selling more produce per store than company-owned ones and resented paying royalty fees (part of their franchise agreement) to what they perceived to be an ineffective brand owner.

Franchisees felt that Heublein was too corporate for their liking and a battle over contracts ensued. The management team was determined to rely on the positive relationships that had been built in the past, despite a number of disputes over contracts and a breakdown in communication.

Consequently, the brand's image began to suffer in the public eye and turnaround plans began in earnest, both on the physical identity of the business and its core offering – fried chicken. Efforts were made to revert to Harland's original cooking methods and the menu was scaled down to reduce costs. Sadly, Harland died in 1980 from leukaemia, and was unable to see the transformation take effect.

New horizons

Going back to basics helped to lift the business' fortunes and culminated in an advertising campaign, 'We do chicken right', that proved so successful it ran for seven years. In 1982, parent company Heublein was acquired by RJ Reynolds Industries, which provided a vital cash injection, a platform for further international expansion and a new vision for the business. That year, sales reached an impressive $2.4bn, largely credited to the fact that the business refused to imitate competitors and introduce a flurry of new products, concentrating instead on refining its existing proposition.

The advertising campaign, 'We do chicken right' proved so successful it ran for seven years

It was a turnaround that did not go unnoticed by food and beverage giant PepsiCo and in 1986, keen to secure a large market for its own drinks, it acquired Kentucky Fried

HOW **THEY** STARTED

Chicken for $840m (£504m), impressed by the latter's increase in worldwide revenues. It seemed a natural fit, too, as PepsiCo already owned fellow fast-food chains Taco Bell and Pizza Hut.

The new owners wanted to continue to develop the business, and therefore opened the Colonel Sanders Technical Centre to foster product development. The business experimented with the concept of oven-roasted chicken and a home delivery model. It also set its sights on further global expansion, culminating with the opening of an outlet in the People's Republic of China in 1987 – the first US fast-food chain to establish a presence in the country.

On the outside, the business appeared to have got back on track but relationships with franchisees in the USA were still strained. Although they were impressed with their new owner's expertise and access to international markets, many American franchisees felt they did not have enough say in the business compared to 20 years ago. Competitors were also developing new product lines and Kentucky Fried Chicken struggled to innovate the fried chicken concept, with Hot Wings and sandwich-style chicken its only new offerings.

It was a different story globally, however, as international markets continued to thrive, both on the financial and franchisee relationship side, with pre-tax profits of $92m (£46m) in 1992, as opposed to $86m (£43m) in the USA. Sales in Asia and operations in Australia were particularly strong and the company seized the opportunity to capitalise on this, with plans to open an outlet outside of the USA every day. Innovations introduced in global operations were often used as a model for entering new markets.

Where are they now?

Amid growing concerns about the health risks associated with fried foods in 1991, the business changed its name to KFC. PepsiCo sold KFC to Yum Restaurants International, along with its other fast-food businesses in 2002. The business continues to thrive today, adjusting its product range as demand from customers' moves – in the last three years the company has removed all trans fats from its products, and Kentucky Grilled Chicken has just been launched in North America.

It may be just under 40 years since Harland Sanders died, but his standards and belief in the product have lived on through the years. His secret recipe is one that is guarded closely even today, locked away in a vault in Louisville, Kentucky. Only a handful of people know what goes into the recipe and they are sworn to secrecy. Meanwhile millions of people enjoy the Colonel's products every day, right across the world.

Pizza Hut

A SLICE OF HISTORY

Founders: **Dan and Frank Carney**

Age of founders at start: **27 and 20**

Background: **College students, working in a grocery store**

Year of foundation: **1958**

Business type: **Pizza restaurant and takeaway**

Countries now trading in: **100**

Turnover and profit: **Not available**

HOW **THEY** STARTED

I f you have ever ordered a takeaway pizza or eaten it in a restaurant, then it's likely you've come across Pizza Hut. Established 50 years ago in the USA, the business is now the world's largest pizza company, with 6,200 sites in the USA and more than 4,000 across the world, spread over 100 countries.

Split into two types of restaurant – a family dining-style eatery and a fast-food concept under the Pizza Hut Express brand – the business is as well known for its creative crusts as it is for its pizza. It's certainly a household name today but the idea for the business sprung from much more modest roots, sparked off by an article on pizza in a New York newspaper.

Humble beginnings

Brothers Dan and Frank Carney were both studying at college in Wichita, Kansas, USA, in the 1950s when a friend suggested it would be a good idea to open a pizza parlour. He'd read an article in *The New York Post* on how the dough-based product was becoming popular on the East Coast. Pizza was a rarity at the time and was certainly unheard of in the Kansas region but the enthusiastic brothers decided to give it a go, despite the fact that they didn't have a clue how to make pizza.

They were in part also spurred on by advice from their late father who had told Dan that 'if you ever have a choice, be in business for yourself, because you get the satisfaction that you know if you fail or you win, it's yours and you don't have somebody over you who's not giving you good opportunities to succeed'. Dan had grown up working in the family grocery store but that was as close as he had come thus far to starting a business, until this opportunity presented itself.

Keeping it in the family, the brothers persuaded their mother to loan them $600 ($4,500 or £2,552). As they weren't even sure how to make a pizza, they did the next best thing and went in search of someone who did. This led to a partnership with John Bender, a serviceman who had worked in the pizza industry in Indiana. John came up with the recipe which was slightly modified by Dan and Frank to include 'a handful of this and a handful of that', and the rest of their funds were used to rent premises and buy second-hand equipment to make pizzas.

Coming up with the business name was slightly easier. The building had a sign that only allowed for eight letters and a space – adamant that the word 'pizza' would be used, the brothers had to come up with another word containing only three letters. Dan's wife suggested that the building looked like a hut and the business – and its iconic name – took shape.

Dan's wife suggested that the building looked like a hut and the business – and its iconic name – took shape

A MODERN PIZZA HUT RESTAURANT

Pizza sensation

The first restaurant, seating up to 25 people, and serving beer and pizza, opened in 1958. The Carneys gave away pizzas for free on opening night in order to drum up interest. Business was brisk, with many of the 10-inch and 14-inch-sized pizzas ordered as takeaways. Letting customers sample the produce before buying had been a prudent move – interest was sparked in the local community, and for many, a visit to Pizza Hut was the first time they had ever tasted pizza. Long queues formed to sample the baked dough with its fresh toppings and herbs.

Not even the brothers could have predicted just how tasty the prospects would be, both in terms of the product and the potential for expansion. The business was originally intended to provide income to finance Frank's undergraduate course and Dan's postgraduate education, but surprised all by yielding high profits on weekly sales of around $1,500 ($11,000 or £6,000 today). Rent, at $135 a month, accounted for the business' largest overhead. Based on this formula and the local community's new-found appetite for pizza, the company's popularity soared, so much so that they opened a second outlet with a takeaway service just a few months later.

Letting customers sample the produce before buying had been a prudent move . . . for many, a visit to Pizza Hut was the first time they had ever tasted pizza

But it wasn't just the customers who were tempted. Other restaurant managers were impressed with the business potential, wanting to be a part of the company and operate a similar restaurant. This prompted the Carneys to turn to a franchising model in the 1960s to expand the business outside of Kansas City and to cater for growing interest from restaurants. It was a different story, however, with the Wichita banks who offered the brothers little support, doubting the profitability of such a franchise concept. Undaunted and in typical entrepreneurial fashion, the brothers went ahead with their expansion through franchise plans, using their own funds. A year and a half later, they had incorporated the business and boasted five Pizza Hut outlets, comprising four company owned sites, and their first franchise opened by Dick Hussar in Topeka, Kansas, which the brothers partly financed.

Growing pains

The first franchise marked the start of ambitious growth plans. Many of the early franchisees were college friends who had helped the Carneys at the beginning and who had acquired a taste for the business. The brothers, however, were not yet focusing on how the business would develop in the long term. They still regarded franchising very much as a short-term prospect, to help finance their education, which they had put on hold for a while (Frank eventually got his degree in 2000, putting it on hold for over four decades!). In a later interview, Frank observed that 'more than trying to develop a chain of international restaurants, we were helping a friend. That is the way franchising proceeded over the next three or four years.'

He added that it was perhaps not the smartest way to approach business growth, as it meant there was little consistency across the brand and many premises were chosen on the basis that they were inexpensive to turn around, rather than for their suitability for the growing brand. But the early success continued, and the Carneys recognised that the concept could have a life beyond funding tuition.

A slice of a franchise

They decided to grow the business more aggressively, and Pizza Hut started to sign up lots more franchisees to open new outlets. The beauty of the franchising model is that the master franchisor (the original Pizza Hut company) doesn't provide any cash for each new franchise (each franchisee funds their own outlet), which enables it to grow without needing substantial extra capital. Pizza Hut made money by supplying each franchise with ingredients, equipment, training, the brand name, and by receiving a small percentage of the sales as a franchise fee. They began franchising the Pizza Hut name for an initial fee of $100 ($650 or £348 today) and a monthly royalty of $100.

In keeping with their entrepreneurial spirit, the brothers also kept a close eye on the competition. They believed that Shakey's Pizza, a chain that was developing a strong presence along the West Coast, would soon challenge their territory. They decided to strengthen the image of Pizza Hut as a neighbourhood eatery and ensure that additional chains and buildings were standardised to provide a united front to counter the competition.

The brothers also strengthened their hold on the business, buying out the interest held by Bender. By 1966, franchises numbered 145, in addition to their six company-owned outlets, having grown through a network of friends and business colleagues, prompting the brothers to set up a home office in Wichita to monitor business growth. By now these all used similar red-roofed buildings and internal layouts, ensuring that customers became familiar with the brand's look and feel. Not content with growing the business on a national basis, the Carneys also had their sights set on the bigger picture, and two years later, in 1968 the first Canadian franchise opened its doors. Franchising was growing rapidly in North America at this time, as it provided thousands of people with an easy way to pursue 'the American dream' and run their own business: at the peak of Pizza Hut's expansion, a new restaurant was being launched every day.

At the end of Pizza Hut's first decade in business, the chain had grown to 310 locations, serving more than a million people weekly.

> By now all the franchises used similar red-roofed buildings and internal layouts, ensuring that customers became familiar with the brand's look and feel

The company set up The International Pizza Hut Franchise Holders Association (IPHFA) to acquire 40% of the company's franchise operations, adding these to the six sites wholly owned by the business, to try to get a more even balance between company sites and franchisees. There seemed to be no stopping the growth of Pizza Hut and on the advice of a business acquaintance, Martin Hart (who went on to invest in rival pizza business Papa John's), Dan and Frank prepared the company for a public listing in 1969 to raise finance for further expansion.

Back to basics

The integration of franchises, however, proved to be a tall order and did not run as smoothly as Dan and Frank would have wished. Previous franchise owners had used various accounting systems and merging all of these into one bigger system became a long drawn-out process, taking nearly a year to complete and creating something of an operational nightmare. Although the public offering raised around $6m, the knock-on effect on the business of integrating the accounting systems was telling, as the brothers lost their focus on marketing and growth: sales flattened and profits took a hit. Pizza Hut had by then established itself as the number one pizza restaurant chain in the world in terms of both turnover and number of restaurants, but it was going to have to work hard to maintain that position.

A radical overhaul of the business looked likely, and the brothers decided to implement a long-term business plan to help get the business back on track, which involved some refranchising. In an interview in 1972, Frank said: 'We about lost control of the operations. Then we figured out that we had to learn how to plan! This included strengthening the management team, increasing sales and profit, tapping into emerging and growing markets and identifying potential business opportunities. One of these was product diversification – Pizza Hut expanded through an 80% stake in frozen pizza crust manufacturer Ready Italy and also formed a joint venture with Sunflower Food Processors, adding sandwiches alongside its thin-crust pizzas.

National restaurant openings flourished and the business celebrated its 1,000th restaurant opening in Wichita, Kansas. The company grew further with the purchase of three other restaurant divisions, Taco Kid, Next Door and the Flaming Steer, as well as the acquisition of a restaurant supply company and a food and supplies distributor. A firm presence was also established on a global basis – by 1976, the 100th international Pizza Hut restaurant had opened its doors in Australia, following earlier openings in other far-flung locations such as Japan, Costa Rica and the UK. By this time, the entire network of Pizza Hut outlets had swelled to 2,000. With the business promoting a more confident outlook alongside its trademark red roofs, company-owned stores continued to grow, seating between 60 and 120 people, and Pizza Hut raised further funds to support this growth through a series of additional stock market share offerings. One of the beauties of the stock market is that a company which is doing well can raise additional funds to grow easily.

With the business promoting a more confident outlook alongside its trademark red roofs, company-owned stores continued to grow, seating between 60 and 120 people

Peak performance

Aggressive marketing and innovative advertisements were key to both international growth and national recognition. They were central to Pizza Hut's growing popularity and this strategy continued throughout the 1960s and 1970s. The brand's first television commercial, developed in 1965, was a musical jingle based on the words 'Putt Putt to the Pizza Hut'. Campaigns were run on both a national and regional level and the level of importance attached to advertising was evident in the budget allocated – it increased from $942,000 (£377,000) in 1972 to just over $3m (£1.2m) two years later.

Advertising didn't just raise the public profile of the company – it also attracted the attention of global food and beverage company PepsiCo to the point where it offered to buy Pizza Hut. In 1977, the brothers sold their shares in a deal that saw PepsiCo pay $320m (£160m) in stock to Pizza Hut shareholders. As the brothers owned 10%, they received $32m ($115m or £61m today) – a substantial amount for the time and more than enough to cover any future tuition costs! Pizza Hut became a division of PepsiCo, with sales that year breaking through the $400m (£200m) barrier.

A parting of the ways beckoned for the brothers – Frank stayed on with the business for three years in the role of chairman but Dan decided the time was right to move on. In an interview in 2002, he said: 'I think I'm an entrepreneur. I enjoy building things up or trying to build them up, and once it becomes old hat, large business, I don't like it either from the top or from the bottom. It's not fun. I thought it was ideal for me that I could turn around and sell and walk away.'

In 1980, Frank too left the business, and although his departure meant the Carney name was no longer associated with Pizza Hut, the brothers' legacy lived on. Before he left Pizza Hut, Frank helped to create one of the restaurant's best-loved products, the Personal Pan Pizza, a pizza in a smaller, single-serving size. 'I can now say that pizza is in my blood,' recalled Frank. 'It is where I've had the most fun.' It was a product he found hard to distance himself from. After leaving Pizza Hut, Frank had numerous offers from pizza companies eager to tap into his expertise, but he consciously avoided pizza, making investments in companies as diverse as real estate, oil and gas exploration as well as automotive businesses. But the pizza temptation was to prove too strong and Frank eventually joined Pizza Hut's fledgling rival Papa John's as a franchisee. In recent years, he has grown a substantial stake in the business, while Dan went on to work as a venture capitalist, keen to spot new business opportunities.

PIZZA HUTS' ITALIAN-STYLE PIZZA: THE COMPANY IS CONSTANTLY INNOVATING ITS PRODUCTS

Beating the competition

It was clear that PepsiCo had spotted a golden opportunity in its acquisition of Pizza Hut, as an increasing number of people were choosing to eat outside their homes. But a host of competitors emerged to cater for this boom in fast-food restaurant-style eating and Pizza Hut suddenly had to fight for customers alongside other pizza providers, such as Domino's, PizzaExpress and Little Caesar.

Inspired by its parent company's marketing background, Pizza Hut decided to create a number of branded products to help its brand stand out from the crowd. It promoted lines such as its Pan Pizza and introduced other ideas, including its Hand-Tossed Traditional Pizza, launched in 1988, and special lunch deals. In the meantime, a new management team was appointed, with Steven Reinemund becoming president and chief executive in 1984. This heralded a period of substantial growth for the business – in 1986, the 5,000th Pizza Hut opened for business and a home-delivery business was launched too. This proved to be a hugely successful move as a few years later, in the early 1990s, deliveries and takeaways accounted for a quarter of Pizza Hut sales.

Pizza Hut decided to create a number of branded products to help its brand stand out from the crowd

The restaurant chain, meanwhile, was still focused on furthering its presence globally and penetrating new markets to gain further competitive advantage, with a restaurant opening in Moscow in 1990. This spawned a Russian pizza, the Moskva, a version topped with tuna, mackerel, salmon and onion. Performance on a global scale was promising – the Russian branch was Pizza Hut's highest performing unit in terms of volume, with Hong Kong, France, Finland and the UK also posting strong results. Key to the success of these global ventures was tapping into the tastes of individual markets – consumers in Hong Kong and Canada for example appeared to favour corned beef and bacon toppings respectively, while curry pizzas were popular with those in Australia.

But the competition refused to go away and in the early 1990s, Pizza Hut faced its toughest test yet, when fast-food burger chain McDonalds launched a rival product – the McPizza – in several test markets, and also offered a home delivery option. The fact that Pizza Hut withstood this challenge and even upped its profits by 10% was testament to the business' strength and the loyalty of its customers. Pizza Hut also benefited from consumers' increased interest in healthy eating, where they perceived pizza as an alternative to other fast-food options that were greasy or fried as well as garnering a following from the growing number of people choosing to follow a vegetarian diet (most burger bars didn't offer salad bars).

Access all areas

Capitalising on the growth of fast food and convenience options was Pizza Hut's next gamble. It spent most of the 1990s developing drive-through outlets and opening stores within shopping centres, which became known as Pizza Hut Express. It was a strategy that paid off as the business increasingly spread to non-traditional locations such as sports arenas and school cafeterias to cope with demand.

Staying true to its original roots as a local pizza eatery, the business also forged links with the community through one of the earliest cause-related marketing initiatives, Book-It, a national reading programme incentive programme which launched in 1984 with 200,000 elementary school students enrolled. By the 1990s, nearly 17 million students in North America alone were involved and the business received an endorsement from George Bush, the US president at the time. The company also became an internet pioneer, when in 1994, it became the first national chain to let customers in a test area within California order takeaway pizza over the internet.

Strengthening the business' global presence continued to be a priority and by 1997, the chain had spread to 90 countries, buoyed by consumers' passion for eating out and convenience foods. But ongoing investment in new outlets was proving to be a strain on the company's resources, and it also had to contend with aggressive price cuts from rivals and a pizza market that was stagnant rather than booming. Sales in restaurants that had opened within the last year fell by several per cent, contributing to an overall drop in company sales of around 21%.

HOW **THEY** STARTED

It was time for a change in direction and Pizza Hut went back to what it did best –
creating innovative products to tempt consumers back to the brand. These included a
stuffed crust pizza with mozzarella cheese baked inside, buffalo wings and Totally New
Pizzas, which contained more toppings than previous ones and thicker sauces. Products
were heavily backed by advertising campaigns, featuring celebrities such as Ringo Starr,
Donald and Ivana Trump and Muhammad Ali. Initial results were promising – Pizza Hut's
market share rose and sales in 1995 increased by 16%, with the stuffed crust setting
company sales records.

PepsiCo took the decision to combine the back office operations of its three restaurant
brands, Pizza Hut, Taco Bell and KFC. In 1997, this was spun off into a specific restaurant
division, Tricon Global Restaurants, which in 2002 joined food brands Long John Silver's
and A&W restaurants to become part of Yum! Brands.

Where are they now?

Over the last few years, Pizza Hut has continued to experiment with new products and
brand extensions against a background of flagging pizza sales. In 2005, an upscale
concept, Pizza Hut Italian Bistro, was created at 50 locations. Food is similar to that
served in Pizza Hut, but with a selection of pasta dishes. At the other end of the scale,
in 2007 they launched Pizza Mia, a pizza product aimed at the more cost-conscious
consumer.

2008 marks Pizza Hut's 50th birthday, and the business is looking onwards and upwards,
expanding its presence in the pasta market in particular. Its gamble with pasta appears
to have paid off. In April, Pizza Hut reported that its newest menu item, Tuscani Pastas,
has become one of the most successful product launches in the company's history.
A makeover is also on the cards as the brand looks to update its look with plasma
televisions and local sports memorabilia. And while the Carney brothers have pursued
other interests, they still keep an eye on their first business startup.

dyson

Dyson

DESIGNING FROM DUST

Founder: **James Dyson**

Age of founder at start: **45**

Background: **Engineer**

Year of foundation: **1992**

Business type: **Technology manufacturer**

Countries now trading in: **45**

Turnover and pre-tax profit: **£514.7m ($980m) and £115m ($220m)**

HOW **THEY** STARTED

That James Dyson sees himself as an inventor first and an entrepreneur second provides a fascinating insight into the motivations of the man behind the iconic Dyson brand. The company's products are now available in 45 countries around the world and Dyson has become a byword for innovative design and high-quality, user-friendly products. His remarkable and inspiring success story can be broken down into two broad stages: the long hard slog to establishing national success and later, a tough but canny business decision that would be the catalyst for Dyson's global success. Entrepreneurs are, by definition, risk takers. Yet many would have balked at James' proposition that he could challenge huge incumbents in the domestic appliance market by competing on innovation instead of price. It's tempting to point to the effectiveness of the firm's marketing, the quality of its manufacturing and distribution strategy or even the stagnation and similarity of the established products from the likes of Hoover, Electrolux and Bosch.

In reality, everything comes back to what James identifies as the 'wow' factor of his products. In the early days he was convinced that word of mouth would do some very significant leg work for his firm if he could just get people to use his revolutionary vacuum cleaners. He was emphatically right, but his journey was a long one. First of all, he would need every ounce of confidence in himself and his venture that he could muster. But if Dyson's foundation required plenty of heart, a test of business nous would be required to catapult its growth and establish Dyson as an international phenomenon.

Early inspiration

One of three children, James Dyson was born in Norfolk in 1947. While studying at the Royal College of Art, he cultivated a dream that he could be a modern day Brunel and revolutionise the way products are designed. He designed his graduation piece, the Sea Truck, for British inventor and entrepreneur Jeremy Fry in 1969.

Jeremy gave James his first job after he graduated at his firm Rotork, promoting him to director just three years later. In this position, James discovered the difficulty of selling the commercially unfinished Sea Truck and learnt the importance of perfecting a design before its production. The product went on to achieve sales of over £263m ($500m) across more than 50 countries, but James left in 1974 to pursue his own inventions, including the award-winning Ballbarrow, a deviation from the wheelbarrow, using a pneumatic ball in place of the usual wheel.

He needed capital to fund his first venture, and persuaded two wealthy people he knew (one who was his brother-in-law) to invest, and Kirk-Dyson was founded. By March 1974 they had a prototype but six months into production the manufacturer they had chosen began raising its prices, leading to a decision to borrow another £45,000 ($104,000), something like £336,000 today, to buy machinery from America and manufacture it themselves. A *Sunday Times* journalist picked up on the invention and they were soon selling 45,000 Ballbarrows annually, turning over £600,000 ($1.4m) The company tried

JAMES WITH THE NOW-FAMOUS DC01

to export its products to America to grow sales, but ended up in a costly lawsuit with an American business which had produced a very similar product after taking on one of James' staff.

During this period, James noticed how the industrial cleaner at the Ballbarrow factory was constantly clogging with dust during production. He found out that he would need to pay £75,000 ($173,000), about £562,500 today ($797,000) to install a cyclone, used for large-scale industrial cleaning. Instead of paying this colossal sum, he designed and built a 30ft industrial cyclone tower, which removed the powder particles by exerting centrifugal forces 100,000 times greater than those of gravity. Wondering if the same process could be made to work in miniature, James took the idea for a vacuum cleaner that wouldn't clog to the Kirk-Dyson board, but was met with pessimism. Financial friction soon led to James being ousted from Kirk-Dyson by the other shareholders. Crucially, Ballbarrow's patent was owned by the company, not the inventor, so James left without his design – a mistake he would never repeat.

Undeterred, he spent the next five years barely managing to survive while producing an almost unbelievable 5,127 prototypes until finally, the world's first bagless vacuum cleaner arrived. His groundbreaking design used two cyclones to separate the dust from the air to stop the machine from clogging. Although he had set up the Air Power Vacuum Cleaner Company five years previously, with the backing of his old friend Jeremy Fry, the lengthy and costly process left the firm deeply in debt and meant it couldn't manufacture the products itself. Changing the company name to Prototypes Ltd, James and Jeremy changed tack, now opting to license the invention to other companies to produce, rather than manufacture it themselves.

His groundbreaking design used two cyclones to separate the dust from the air to stop the machine from clogging

Born of frustration

Several frustrating years ensued. James faced a reluctance to invest in new technology, paltry returns offered by potential manufactures at home and a series of abortive deals with Black & Decker, Comair and Amway in the USA. A deal was actually signed with Amway in April 1984, but within a matter of months it withdrew from the contract, accusing Prototypes Ltd of deceiving it as the product was not yet ready. An eight-month legal battle was to deny James the opportunity to re-license his product elsewhere until early 1985. He settled quickly due to legal costs and had to give back everything Amway had paid him.

By this stage, heavy debts meant that financing the manufacture of his own product was impossible. His only hope was to succeed in licensing his technology to one country to generate an income which he could use to fund his own manufacturing. The change in his fortunes was to come from the most unlikely of sources – Japan, the home of hi-tech. A local manufacturer offered a reasonable deal and James sold the rights to the technology in Japan and at last began manufacturing vacuum cleaners. Known as the 'G Force', the licensed product won the 1991 International Design Fair prize in Japan. The Japanese were so impressed by its performance that it became a status symbol, selling for £1,200 ($2,000) apiece.

This was just the platform Dyson needed. Despite another costly legal battle with Amway, who had begun designing cleaners with a cyclone design, and a distinct lack of interest from investors, James decided to manufacture a new model under his own name in Britain, using income from the Japanese license. He developed a machine that collected even finer particles of dust, dirt, allergens and mould. The result was the DC01, the first in a range of cleaners to give constant suction. Its Dual Cyclone system was the first breakthrough in technology since the invention of the vacuum cleaner in 1901. After the machine's outer cyclone has spun out the larger dust and dirt particles, the inner cyclone accelerates the air still further to remove the minute particles. James' dream of a better product at a price people could afford was closer than ever. But to be able to manufacture, more money was needed, so James decided to sell all the rights to his technology to the manufacturer in Japan. This generated nearly all of the £900,000 ($1.5m) he needed to go into production and Dyson Ltd was born.

Its Dual Cyclone system was the first breakthrough in technology since the invention of the vacuum cleaner in 1901 ... James' dream of a better product at a price people could afford was closer than ever

The new firm's first sale was made in July 1992 to Great Universal Stores, the largest mail order group in Britain. James recalls that after six hours of negotiations, he finally admitted to its chief buyer that he found its catalogue boring and felt it needed an injection of new technology, in the form of his Dyson DC01 cleaner. This risky but candid approach sealed the deal and the catalogue company ordered 1,000 units. James quickly secured orders from more catalogues, including Littlewoods. Initially, he was cautious not to approach the high street retailers in case competitors got wind of the impending launch, but scrapped this strategy when John Lewis asked to take 250 DC01s.

In November 1992, tools and huge moulds were transported to Wales, where Phillips Plastics was to produce the machines. The first DC01s rolled off the production line in January 1993. In April, a big order from electrical goods retailer Rumbelows set Dyson up with a solid base of orders. The future looked rosy but when Phillips suddenly hiked its prices, Dyson was forced to gradually move production elsewhere. Yet another lawsuit forced Dyson to stop manufacturing for one crucial month. James and his team quickly set up a production factory in an old Royal Mail warehouse and produced the very first DC01 exclusively made by a Dyson Ltd employee in July 1993.

Fifteen painful, long years after his cleaning epiphany, James finally had his own business, manufacturing his revolutionary cleaner. He had spent £1.5m ($2m) on patents and almost £3m ($4m) on development. But the delayed rewards were to be exponential.

HOW **THEY** STARTED

While sales grew steadily at first, when superstores Comet and Currys started to sell the machine in 1995, the DC01 quickly became the bestselling vacuum cleaner in the UK, where it has stayed ever since. By January 1997 Dyson was selling more vacuum cleaners than Hoover and Electrolux combined.

DYSON'S RESEARCH, DESIGN AND DEVELOPMENT CENTRE AT MALMESBURY

Going global

When Dyson was having its spot of bother with Phillips, James opened a research centre and factory in Malmesbury, Wiltshire, not far from his home, which was to play a significant part in Dyson's global story. The firm was the largest single employer in the town by a long way, and its population had played a key role in driving the company's belated British success story. But the relationship hasn't always run smoothly.

'The company had been expanding pretty much from the word go,' says Martin McCourt, the man James hired as chief operating officer in a shrewd move in 1996. 'It expanded in the first three years very much as a UK company with a very small proportion of its business coming from overseas.' When Dyson began to move into European markets and Japan, Australia and New Zealand between 1996 and 1999, a demand for a wider range of Dyson products for different needs was created.

While a number of new product launches – including the world's first washing machine with two drums rotating in opposite directions for a quicker, more thorough wash in 2000 – kept the popularity of the brand growing throughout the late 1990s and beyond, profits in 2001 and 2002 were lower than expected. The cause? Put simply, the escalating cost of manufacturing in Britain coupled with a lack of available space to build extra production capacity. Reluctantly, the company had to rein in expansion while setting up small production lines in Birmingham to cope with demand – a very inefficient way to manufacture. Dyson had run out of space.

'We were running from our factory in Malmesbury 24 hours a day, seven days a week. We couldn't squeeze another single vacuum cleaner out. Our preference was to expand in the area that we were in,' says Martin.

This option was met with a firm 'no' from the local authorities. The fear was that the small, already Dyson-dominated West Country market town would lose its identity. 'People took the view that we were successful enough. They thought our expansion would spoil a rural community.'

Martin and his team started considering alternatives, namely off-shoring. Any company entwined with its locality, and with a reasonably high profile, will recognise it was not a decision to be taken lightly. But it was hard to ignore the advantages, says Martin. 'If we were to move to a lower-cost production line but also one where there was no limit to our capacity, we could solve two significant problems in one go.' The increased production capacity would help fuel all the planned investments in the business and thus prevent the need to seek venture capital.

'There had already been a gravitational shift on the part of our suppliers who gave us the various bits and pieces that we source to make up the Dyson product,' says Martin. 'They had all moved their centre of gravity to the Far East. We were in the ridiculous situation where we were bringing materials from the Far East to the UK, assembling them and sending them back out. It just didn't make sense.' Action was needed. So the difficult decision was made to move production line assembly from Malmesbury to Malaysia in order to expand and stay competitive in an increasingly global market. While keeping Dyson's hub – the research and development centre – in Wiltshire.

A cultural leap

James gave Martin, who had been promoted to chief executive officer in 2001, the task of managing the transition. He chose Johor Bahru, the capital city of Johor in southern Malaysia. Crucial factors in this decision included positive early dealings with its government, a pre-existing infrastructure and the fact that the English language was not a major barrier. Martin's team familiarised themselves with how various government departments worked, ensuring there wouldn't be trouble organising visas for staff posted to Malaysia. 'It was also important to understand how their finances worked in order to respect the local finance and tax regimes. These things are all really important and we haven't fallen foul,' he says.

Japanese electronics companies and Hewlett-Packard had been active in the area, leaving behind a high-quality, reliable manufacturing base. 'A lot of these guys had already begun to evacuate and were off to China, so we were able to take up some of the production capacity,' says Martin. 'Most Malaysians speak English, making the transition easier, because there was no language barrier. It was quite a comfortable cultural leap and much easier than I thought it would be.'

Red tape has proved relatively light, too. While, inevitably, there's a level of bureaucracy, the company has been able to expand efficiently, opening new factories within a six-month timescale. It started with two main factories in Johor Bahru, quickly grew to three and now stands at five, albeit including the Dyson Digital Motor Factory, which is in neighbouring Singapore.

Back home of course, the decision wasn't popular. James took flak from the national press as well as Wiltshire's locals. So how did the firm handle that process? 'We did everything that we could reasonably do to assist those people who we couldn't retain to find alternative employment,' Martin explains. 'I'm pleased to say that every single person who wanted to work somewhere else managed to find alternative employment. We set up a working group with local authorities including the local council to help them do just that. We helped with structuring CVs and interview practice – we did what we thought was the right thing to do.'

It was a tough decision, but it wasn't a ruthless one. Ultimately, it was dramatically vindicated. Pre-tax profits were over £46m ($736m) for 2003, up from £20.4m ($32.6m) the previous year. 'We now have more people working in Malmesbury than we did at the time of that transfer and we have three times more people working around the Dyson world.

'The move to Malaysia lifted the lid off our expansion. We were able to develop new factories very quickly and we were able to remove any constraints on capacity. We were able to raise our quality standards because we were able to use people who were much more experienced than we were in manufacturing. And we were able to generate additional cash which assisted us in expanding to markets like Japan and America.'

> 'We now have more people working in Malmesbury than we did at the time of that transfer and we have three times more people working around the Dyson world'

Success in an expanding market

Recounting this part of the tale makes it sound remarkably easy compared with the protracted struggle of the early years. 'The end result makes it look smooth but it didn't feel like that when we were going through it', Martin recalls. 'It's an enormous undertaking. We were transferring our manufacturing operation to the Far East and at the same time we were involved in a startup project in the USA as well as developing all of our European markets and designing new products for launch in Japan.' So what's the secret of multi-tasking a global expansion of this scale? 'The challenge was really about a relatively small group of people managing and driving quite a complex growth strategy. It's great fun and it's very exhilarating but it's very hard work. By making sure that the plan is very clear and that you're doing the right thing, you execute the plan well. If you haven't got the right people around you, you'll mess up. If you have, it will happen' says Martin.

And it really did happen, in an impressive fashion. The US market opened up at just the right time to coincide with the company's increased capacity, with Dyson getting its rights for North America back from the Toronto Courts in December 2001. It launched there in October 2002, just as the transfer completed. Japan also rocketed. The company spent seven years and a good part of £11m ($20m) researching and developing a more powerful and smaller product, the DC12, specifically for that market. 'We shifted 200,000 vacuum cleaners in Japan in a year. Western domestic companies don't usually do that. And we made money – and they don't usually do that either,' says Martin.

He estimates that Dyson now produces around twice as many products as it had pre-transfer, all funded by earnings in the USA and the other 45 countries it now trades in.

While operating in so many territories undoubtedly requires some rather complex logistical operations, the company's strategy for establishing and promoting the brand remains largely unchanged. 'The method that we've used has been virtually identical, market after market, Martin says. 'James' method is as simple as it is effective. It started with a product idea that was just significantly better than anything else. It wasn't about advertising, marketing or even PR. It was about people getting their hands on the product, using it and thinking "wow".

> *'James' method is as simple as it is effective. It started with a product idea that was just significantly better than anything else.'*

'When I met James, I saw studies that said that 80% of the Dyson products being bought in the UK at that time were bought because of recommendation by a family member or friend. That has been repeated in America and that should be your starting point. If you don't have a product that works differently and better than all of the others, you're not going to get that. Why would people talk about it? All the advertising and PR campaigns in the world won't create word of mouth unless your product is inherently better.'

The wow factor

The two key factors that transformed a parochial success story into an international phenomenon, Martin says, were gaining a foothold in the USA and moving the manufacturing base. 'Everything has doubled since that time – volumes, revenue, profits (more than doubled). All the key factors in the business responded brilliantly. Before the move, less than a third of our business came from overseas; now it's two-thirds. We're also holding the number one or two positions in the majority of markets we're in, including America. It was obviously regrettable we had to take that decision, but it has propelled us onto the world stage.'

ALWAYS INNOVATING – THE DCI 6, A HANDHELD VACUUM CLEANER THAT DOESN'T LOSE SUCTION

Innovation is still at the heart of everything Dyson does, and almost half of the firm's research and development (R&D) spend goes on products that aren't directly related to its core offering. In 2006, it launched a product that looks set to do for hand dryers what the DC01 did for vacuum cleaners. 'The Dyson Airblade™ hand dryer is a perfect and recent example of the way that we view product development, technology and our identity as a company,' says Martin. 'Everybody who uses toilet facilities has experienced using an electrical hand dryer. Few of us would comment on that process productively. You've got a problem, but you haven't got the world at large wondering around moaning about electrical hand dryers. It's back of mind, not front of mind. That's perfect Dyson territory.'

Breaking all of the conventions again, unlike a conventional hand dryer, the Dyson Airblade™ hand dryer doesn't generate heat. 'The air scrapes the water off your hands with the air coming at you at 400mph from a tiny gap either side of your hands. No heat involved, simple as that. When someone uses that in a public toilet, they have a 'wow' reaction to how well it works,' Martin explains. And James doesn't make a habit of repeating mistakes, so it's completely protected by patents.

For budding entrepreneurs, the Dyson story is both inspirational and bracing. 'Getting your homework right, particularly when you're straying beyond your comfort zone which might be your home market, is crucial, as is knowing how much it will cost you so you don't get a nasty fright,' Martin advises. 'Ensure that you've got your product right. That's the hardest for companies to achieve. A great product that's well designed, well made and does what it's supposed to do will stand out and will be in with an enormous chance of success.'

> 'A great product that's well designed, well made and does what it's supposed to do will stand out and will be in with an enormous chance of success'

Where are they now?

In 2008, Dyson continues to innovate. In March, Dyson launched a new range of Dyson Ball™ machines which use a ball instead of wheels so they can turn on the spot; making them more manoeuvrable. Dyson also released two new cylinder machines, the DC22 and DC23, which use new core separator technology that separates even more microscopic particles from the airflow.

Dyson continues to expand into new territories. The company launched in Canada in 2006 to great success and now sells vacuum cleaners in 45 countries worldwide.

Volvo Cars Corporation

DRIVEN TO SUCCEED

Founders: Assar Gabrielsson and Gustaf Larson

Age of founders at start: 34 and 37

Background: Gabrielsson was an economist and Larson an engineer – they met while at SKF (Swedish Ball Bearing Co)

Year of foundation: 1925

Business type: Automotive

Countries now trading in: 110

Net sales: £13,250m ($24,740m) (first half of 2008)

HOW **THEY STARTED**

V olvo is one of the world's best-known car manufacturers, renowned for the safety of its cars, and for being Swedish. Over its 81-year history, Volvo has had to adapt its offering to remain competitive, but while the technology has evolved, the business has maintained its core brand values of transporting people in an affordable and safe manner. Global expansion has played a leading role in Volvo's success: with a relatively small home market in Sweden, unlike most of its international rivals, the company has always had to view overseas markets as essential rather than optional.

The early days

In 1925 Assar Gabrielsson and Gustaf Larson, as ambitious and proud Swedish nationals, went on a mission to prove they could produce a Swedish car to rival the foreign cars already on the market.

Gabrielsson and Larson met while working for Swedish ball bearing company SKF, where Gabrielsson, a graduate of Stockholm School of Economics, worked in a number of senior sales positions, including export director. Larson was an engineer, who had worked for the British automotive industry for several years before returning to Sweden. Their skills complemented each other's, and armed them well for their mission to commercialise their dream. While Gabrielsson had the economic know-how (and was in a position to secure

THE FOUNDERS, GABRIELSSON AND LARSON OUTSIDE OF A VOLVO GARAGE

the necessary backing), Larson knew how to design a car. In fact, they were obsessed with the idea of building a car of their own to challenge the imported cars that were sold in Sweden at the time.

'It was all very humble beginnings,' says Volvo Cars Heritage manager Claes Rydholm. 'SKF, reluctant at first, was eventually talked into backing them financially, supplied the registered company name Volvo and arranged for the first factory and office facilities. Gabrielsson put all his savings into the venture, SEK 150,000 (Swedish kronor), which in today's money would amount to more than £300,000 ($560,000). In total SKF stumped up approximately SEK 1m, plus the share-capital of SEK 200,000.'

The deal allowed the founders to develop their car using the name of SKF's subsidiary, AB Volvo (literally meaning 'I roll' in Latin), which began life in 1925 making and selling ball and roller bearings for the automotive industry.

Note that this was long before the days of the large car factories, with cars assembled almost entirely by hand, which made it possible for a modest business to even contemplate starting to make cars – something most entrepreneurs wouldn't even consider possible today.

THE PROUD MOMENT ON 14 APRIL 1927, WHEN THE FIRST VOLVO CAR – THE ÖV4 – ROLLED OUT OF THE FACTORY

HOW **THEY** STARTED

Gabrielsson and Larson went on a mission to prove they could produce a Swedish car to rival the foreign cars already on the market

The pair came up with a design for their first car, and built some prototypes. Cars from the first series of AB Volvo's 10 prototypes were sold to business friends as samples, so when the first series-produced cars rolled out of the Gothenburg factory on 14 April 1927, there were already Volvo 'dealers' established in Stockholm and Gothenburg. The original model, which they called the ÖV4, was an 'open tourer' with a four-cylinder engine, priced at SEK 4,800 – the equivalent of £9,000 ($17,000) today. They quickly added a second model, the PV4 saloon, priced at SEK 5,800.

The aim was to build and sell 500 of each model, but Swedish customers were harder to lure than expected and only 297 were sold in the first year. Despite missing their self-imposed target, to sell 300 cars in that first year represented a phenomenal achievement.

This was the golden era of car manufacturing, with developments and new ideas coming thick and fast. The fledgling car manufacturer continued to grow and develop rapidly, and within another year had launched both a lengthened version of the ÖV4 saloon and the company's first truck.

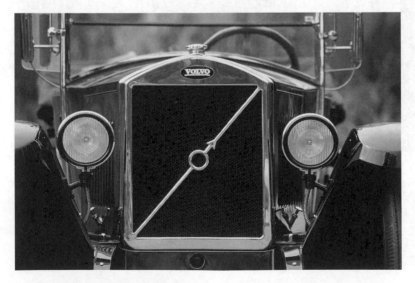

A FRONT SHOT OF THE 1927 ÖV4

A flying start

This dramatic initial growth was a sign of things to come and, by focusing initial marketing efforts on magazines and newspapers, they managed to create quite a buzz around the story of two men building the first Swedish car. So, despite missing sales targets, by the end of year one turnover was SEK 1.4m (or £2m ($3.7m) in today's money) and they had already taken on around 250 employees. What's more, while the brand was inherently Swedish, the founders knew that global expansion would be a key growth strategy and so work began on this at a very early stage. 'In order to survive with a relatively small home market like Sweden, export was of vital importance. This was understood from the very beginning,' says Rydholm.

And so Volvo began exporting in 1928, when it set up its first subsidiary in Finland. It was sensible to start with another country fairly close to home and which did not have its own car marque already there, and this operation worked well. This set the precedent for a rapid rate of growth which has shown no signs of abating over Volvo's 81-year history. By 1929, as well as turning a profit for the first time, the company had developed its first six-cylinder model and sold a total of 1,383 vehicles. Twenty-seven of these were exported, to destinations including Argentina and Palestine, and by the following year Volvo had enough funds to buy the Hisingen factory where its cars were made for parent company SKF.

The founders knew that global expansion would be a key growth strategy and so work began on this at a very early stage

The founders continued to expand their range, and by 1931, they had developed and launched four taxi models. And, despite the worldwide economic depression having an impact on car sales, Volvo managed to thrive, holding onto its 8% market share. In fact, the company paid its first dividend to shareholders this year and also bought a controlling stake in its engine supplier, AB Pentaverken in Skövde, Sweden.

Product development and sales growth continued at a fast pace. A year later, Volvo had produced its 10,000th vehicle and the company began manufacturing cars for the Swedish police. They even produced a series of seven-seater taxis with a high roof which allowed the more distinguished passengers to keep their hats on.

Meanwhile, as predicted and planned, exporting became a vital revenue stream for the business. 775 of the 2,984 vehicles Volvo sold in 1934 were exported, and it was around this time that the company was able to buy out SKF's remaining stake in the business. In 1935, just a year later, shares in Volvo were floated on the Swedish stock exchange.

HOW **THEY** STARTED

Overcoming challenges

Volvo continued its rapid pace of evolution in the years running up to the Second World War, releasing new models each year, but fuel and materials shortages were an immediate problem when the war broke out. Petrol rationing had an effect on unit sales, which fell sharply from 7,306 in 1939 to 5,900 in 1940. However, in a sign of things to come in terms of the company's forward-thinking approach, Volvo was able to start making units which ran on a low-grade fuel called producer gas within a month or two of the start of the war (having already carried out research into petrol alternatives). During the course of the war, the company manufactured tens of thousands of these units. Sales of these and army vehicles helped make up for lost revenue from car sales. Moreover, despite wartime challenges, AB Volvo was still able to make several successful acquisitions, including the purchase of the majority shareholding in Svenska Flygmotor AB. This would later become Volvo Aero, a subsidiary that makes engines and other parts for passenger planes, fighter jets and rockets.

In 1944, Volvo's two 'peacetime cars' went on show at a major exhibition in Stockholm, attracting almost 150,000 people. In two weeks, 2,300 people placed orders for one of the models, the PV444, lured by the SEK 4,800 price tag (the price of the first car in 1927). Following a drawn-out strike in the engineering industries, these were eventually delivered in 1947. The 1947 retail price of a PV444 was SEK 8,000, and Volvo made a loss on the first 2,300. Even so, by now the company had 3,000 employees and an annual turnover of SEK 112m. The next two years saw the growth accelerate following the end of the war: in 1949 Volvo sold its 100,000th vehicle, of which 2,000 had been exported, and the number of people it employed rose to 6,000.

Growing strong

This tremendous growth continued, and by the early 1950s, turnover leapt to SEK 310m, as the PV444 (now fitted with the new must-have accessory, an external plastic sun visor known as the 'gangster cap') became Sweden's bestselling car, and the company started work on its first estate model. Volvo was now well established in the Nordic countries, many European markets without their own national car manufacturers, the Middle East and South America. In the 1950s Volvo added North America to their export mix, along with European countries with markets dominated by domestic makes including Germany, France and the UK.

However, there were also some failures. In 1954, Volvo unveiled the prototype of the Volvo Sport, an American-inspired two-seater fibreglass body. But, aimed primarily at the export market, it proved not to be a commercial success and when Gunnar Engellau took over as managing director in 1956 he stopped production after just 67 had been made.

Global expansion also brought with it its own unique set of challenges, not least 'finding the right importer or dealer and convincing people to buy a car that has been brought into their country from a small place far away that no one had ever heard of', says Rydholm. In North America in particular, Rydholm adds that some said it would be like trying to sell refrigerators to Eskimos, but Volvo soon proved there was a demand for cars like the PV444 in the USA.

In 1956, Volvo exhibited their PV444 model at the motor show in New York and by the summer as many as 100 American dealers had signed up to sell it. By 1963, rising demand lead to Volvo opening its first foreign assembly plant in Halifax, Canada. Volvo's focus on export markets was paying off: by now, the USA was the company's biggest export market by far, and Volvo had become the fourth-largest imported brand there. The group's turnover had exceeded SEK 2bn and their staff count had grown to more than 20,000.

The USA was the company's biggest export market by far, and Volvo had become the fourth-largest imported brand there

Understandably, exporting has been absolutely fundamental to the company's phenomenal success. 'Export is the very condition for survival, having a home market accounting for less than 15% of the sales volume. This is unique in the business', adds Rydholm.

Building a brand

By the late 1950s Volvo's continued product development (in particular, the PV544, an evolution of the PV444) and successful export strategy had propelled turnover to more than SEK 1bn for the first time.

Over time, the global brand became famous for the same core values everywhere, regardless of the product or market: safety and quality. This was no accident – Volvo's marketing pushed safety as its prime unique selling point, driven by its product development teams' results. The company has always been a safety pioneer; Larson famously said in 1936, 'cars are driven by people. The guiding principle behind everything we make at Volvo, therefore, is, and must remain, safety.' Volvo was the first car maker to fit three-point seat belts as standard equipment in its Amazons and PV544s in 1959. Throughout the 1960s, Volvo made a number of other safety-led product improvements, such as installing power brakes for the first time and producing the first prototype of a rear-facing child seat. Its Volvo 144 model included innovations such as a collapsible steering column and energy-absorbing crumple zones, winning it widespread acclaim in export markets as well as at home, where it was voted Car of the Year in 1965.

HOW **THEY** STARTED

'The guiding principle behind everything we make at Volvo is, and must remain, safety.'

Volvo's safety features have also received widespread global acclaim, including The Swedish Automobile Association's gold medal for safety. In the 1960s, the National Highway Traffic Safety Administration in the USA bought a number of Volvo 240s and used them to set the safety standards against which all new cars on the American market were to be tested. In the 1980s, Volvo received the Prince Michael Road Safety Award for the mechanical seat belt tensioner.

As car accidents, and consumers' awareness of them grew, so the safety elements of Volvo's marketing became more powerful sales points, pushing sales on still further. By the 1970s, Volvo had become the bestselling car brand in Scandanavia, and the USA had overtaken Sweden as Volvo's biggest market; by the 1980s Volvo had grown into the biggest imported brand in the USA. They managed this through a series of attention-grabbing advertising campaigns, backed up by a solid product that exceeded customers' expectations with their focus on quality and safety.

THE NEW XC60, ON SALE DURING THE AUTUMN OF 2008

Volvo began to consider environmental concern as early as the 1960s – another example of their pioneering approach, and one which has become highly significant today. 'Today Volvo Cars is facing the giant challenge of designing the cars of tomorrow that will stand for sustainable mobility in the future,' notes Rydholm. For the company that presented its first Environmental Concept Car back in the 1980s, you suspect this challenge won't be insurmountable. A fully functioning hybrid, the 1980s model used gas turbine, electric motor and high-speed generator technology and received attention across the globe for its significant use of recyclable materials.

Where are they now?

The company's founders, managing director Assar Gabrielsson and technical director Gustaf Larson, remained at the helm until the mid-1950s. In 1999, Volvo Cars was sold to Ford Motor Company for SEK 50bn (£47.5bn/$8bn), to ensure the company's reserves were deep enough to fund future research and development. Meanwhile, the brand name Volvo was put into a holding company, Volvo Trademark Holding AB, which is jointly owned by AB Volvo and Ford, and whose management decides on how the name can be used.

'One of the reasons for the Ford acquisition in 1999 was that Volvo Cars did not have the future economic muscles and power to stay independent in a market (with a 1% market share) with steadily tougher competition and increasing pace of product development,' says Rydholm, who adds that the company's plan now is to ensure its 'long-term survival with products that provide sustainable mobility in an optimum way.'

These days, the Volvo Group comprises Volvo Trucks, Volvo Buses, Volvo Construction Equipment, Volvo Penta, Volvo Aero and Volvo Financial Services. But the brand is still best known for its cars. Since its acquisition by Ford, Volvo Cars has continued to go from strength to strength and has continued to be a pioneer. In 2001, the company presented its own range of environmentally sound diesel engines, the D5 range, with CO_2 emissions 30% lower than those from petrol engines of a similar power output. In 2002, the Volvo XC90 won more awards than any other model had previously in such a short time, and soon gained the highest safety ratings from independent testing bodies in both Europe and the USA.

The business achieved a sales record in 2004, thanks to retail deliveries of just under 460,000 cars, and the company now has production facilities all over the world. As Rydholm concludes: 'Volvo Cars has proved to the world that it is possible to gain success in the competitive automotive market even though you play all your games as the away team; with a home market accounting for less than 15% of the sales volumes, as opposed to the competition which all (with the exception of Saab) have strong home markets that account for their major volumes.'

Dorling Kindersley

PIONEERS IN PUBLISHING

Founders: **Peter Kindersley and Christopher Dorling**

Age of founders at start: **33 and 34**

Background: **Art director and cartographer**

Year of foundation: **1974**

Business type: **Publisher**

Countries now trading in: **60**

Turnover and profit: **Not available**

HOW **THEY** STARTED

With a fresh approach to publishing, Peter Kindersley and Christopher Dorling aimed to introduce heavily illustrated full-colour reference books into what was then a comparably dull market. Begun in 1974, the company's first year turnover reached almost £1m ($2.3m), worth more like £7m ($13m) in today's money – a very respectable amount for a new business. From the start, the UK publishers created a global company – their first deal was in New York, with deals in Europe following shortly afterwards. Over the next 30 years, DK established itself as a leading reference and illustrative publisher, overcoming some major hurdles along the way.

Founder foundations

Trained as a painter, Peter Kindersley left home aged 22 to find his fortune in London. He worked for a small magazine publisher where he learnt the publishing skills which he would rely upon heavily throughout his career. He became art director aged 28 while working at publishing house Thomas Nelson and there met Mitchell and Beazley (who went on to found the eponymous illustrated reference publisher). Together they were heavily involved in the expansion of Thomas Nelson and built up a plethora of contacts. In 1967 Mitchell and Beazley set up with map publishers Philips, and Peter joined them from the outset as art director. The new company flourished but after five years, Peter began to tire of the founders' 'aggressive approach to publishing'. Discontented, he wanted to set up his own publishing house; he recalls that for him, 'necessity was the mother of invention'.

Peter's break away was not amicable, and Mitchell Beazley attempted to stop him setting up a rival company by keeping him on as a company director. Initially, Peter had to set his company up in his wife's name, as it was not until he had been released by Mitchell Beazley that he could be named on the paperwork. Christopher Dorling, a friend from Mitchell Beazley, joined the new venture, which soon became known to the trade as 'DK', bringing his skills in sales and editing to complement Peter's strong visual skills.

Dreaming in colour

They envisaged a publishing company that did not do 'one-off' books but created a series spanning lifestyle issues from gardening and wine lists to children's books. The emphasis from the outset was on producing quality illustrated reference books. While text had traditionally swamped the publishing world, the entrepreneurs wanted to introduce more visually led, image-focused books to create an informative, highly readable resource. With such rich illustration, the founders were aware of how easily the books would translate into different languages, and pursued international sales from the start.

PETER KINDERSLEY ON HIS ORGANIC FARM IN BERKSHIRE WHICH HE NOW RUNS

Christopher Dorling, joined the new venture . . . bringing his skills in sales and editing to complement Peter's strong visual skills

DK was founded in October 1974 from the back room of Peter's south London home. Immediately they took on Christopher Davies, one of the editors from Mitchell Beazley. The three of them could lean on their reputation as some of the founding members of Mitchell Beazley, facilitating initial business, especially with contacts in America and Holland.

Initially, DK was established as a book packager, creating ideas for titles and acting as liaison between the authors and publishing houses. They would then sell the rights to various publishers, print the titles in a bulk run and the books would be published under the respective publishing companies' own names around the globe. By doing this, DK ensured a wider circulation of their titles than would have been possible had they set up as a small publisher in the UK alone. This was a relatively new approach and the founders relied heavily both on their reputations in the book trade and on the quality of their first few titles.

HOW **THEY** STARTED

The founders relied heavily both on their reputations in the book trade and on the quality of their first few titles

At their inception Peter settled on three title ideas to launch with. Stemming from his own interest in evolution, he wrote to well-known author Nigel Calder and commissioned a children's book on evolution: from this, *The Origin of Johnny* was born. Confident that wine was a popular subject, they searched for an author and approached Pamela Vandyke Price who wrote *The Taste of Wine* for them. Vandyke Price was already working with a publisher, yet left to work with DK as she was interested in illustrating her work more heavily, which her 'reticent', traditional publisher did not offer. Lastly, renowned author John Hedgecoe was approached to produce *The Book of Photography*, another interest of Peter's. All three titles would be packed with diagrams and photographs in the heavily illustrated format that people have become accustomed to over the years.

Alternative methods

Armed with these titles, Christopher and Peter attended the international Frankfurt Book Fair in October 1974, but could not afford a stall at the popular industry event. Instead, they set up in a 'very dubious hotel in the red light district' and sent their secretary to the fair to implore people to visit them at the end of their day. They spread the layouts on the bed and sat their visitor down on the only chair in the room to conduct their presentation. They received a small but significant turn out, with publishers visiting as a result of the founders' reputation, and also because of the innovative books DK were offering.

After the fair, due to the strong interest DK had received from publishers, the next step was to finalise the book contracts directly with publishing houses. Peter recalls that as they were well respected by groups of publishers in New York from previous business (Peter was the designer for New York publications *The Joy of Sex* and *Hugh Johnson Wine Atlas* – both huge successes), New York was the logical starting point. With a simple business plan they persuaded the bank to grant them a £10,000 ($23,000) overdraft, the equivalent of £75,000 ($140,000) today, by putting up Peter's house as security, to finance the trip to America. Peter remembers that they did not end up using all of this – indeed, the startup was mostly funded by £17,000 ($40,000) that Peter had been paid when leaving Mitchell Beazley.

Their trip to New York lasted three weeks, and finally, in the weeks before Christmas, they sold all three titles to Random House, meaning they only had to complete one momentous deal. Peter describes this break as the 'little bit of luck that is absolutely essential' when starting a business. They had impressed with their experience, but also had ensured they had strong presentations and good authors behind the titles. On his return from New York, Peter received the news that he had been officially sacked from Mitchell Beazley, meaning he could legally now run the company himself.

Going global with ease

Once the partners had secured their first major deal, they hot-footed it to Holland, Italy and other European countries to sell translation rights to publishing houses. The beauty of highly illustrated books was they could easily be produced in several different languages. This had two significant advantages compared to most books: firstly, translation costs were very low as there were significantly fewer words than text-based books, and secondly, the nature of the printing process meant that if you printed all the text in black, enormous cost savings per copy could be made by printing several different language versions at the same time.

A crucial element of Dorling Kindersley's plan was to spend more money on each book than was normal, producing a much better book. To make this profitable they had to produce lots of different language versions at the same time, spreading the cost of the lavish illustrations across a high quantity of books. This meant printing all the books at the same time, and is called co-edition publishing. Peter argues that this was the key to their success.

As you can imagine, getting half a dozen or so publishers in different countries all agreeing to publish a book at the same time can take quite some doing. Peter explains that it was essential to have the manpower to carry this process out and therefore, as soon as the first samples of the book were ready, DK had to have foreign language speakers on its team to facilitate deals with foreign publishers. This was an excellent move, albeit an unusual one for a British company, as speaking the same language proved a huge advantage in dealing with publishers from other countries. In the first year, DK took on one salesman who spoke five European languages and an excellent Spanish-speaking saleswoman; in contrast, most British publishers had perhaps one person in their sales department who was bilingual. Quickly, DK grew its sales force to about six people who travelled the globe completing deals.

Speaking the same language proved a huge advantage in dealing with publishers from other countries . . . quickly DK grew its sales force

Up in smoke

With some important deals in the bag, DK worked manically to complete the first publications. Just as the Dutch printers had begun work on the books, disaster struck. There was a blazing fire in the printing house; all the DK artwork was ruined. The fire cost them thousands and all their hard work had literally gone up in smoke. Fortunately, the photography had been saved, but all other work needed to be redone. Everyone pulled out all the stops to redo the work, and astonishingly, despite this major hindrance, Peter reports that the books arrived on time in America.

Once published, the success of the three preliminary publications varied. *The Origin of Johnny* was sold to a number of publishers over the world but Peter remembers that overall it 'didn't work'; among themselves *The Taste of Wine* was dubbed 'The Waste of Time'; but *The Book of Photography* took off from the word go. It arrived at a time when the Single Lens Reflex cameras were emerging on the market and 'what you needed was a really good book on how to use them'. The author John Hedgecoe struck gold with his practical, informative blend of illustrations and tips. DK was the first to produce a highly illustrated, practical book on photography. Soon after its publication in spring 1975, companies such as Kodak were getting in contact. Peter describes the whole experience as 'fairly incredible' and without doubt sees the book as the best decision he ever made. This book went on to become a million-copy seller.

Developing DK

A year after its foundation, DK moved to new offices in Covent Garden, central London, where it remained for the next 26 years.

DK's subsequent appearances at the Frankfurt Book Fair differed heavily from their debut. Riled by others pinching DK's ideas, the publisher created a wall around their area and patrons could only enter if invited. Peter recalls how 'people loved it; they felt they were superior'. Again, DK made sure all nationalities were made welcome with tables for each country with a native speaker hosting.

THE DK BUILDING ON THE STRAND, CENTRAL LONDON

Within the next three years, the publishing house produced eight titles, three of which have gone on to become million-copy sellers

Momentously, in 1982 DK became a publisher in their own right in the UK. The first title created under the DK brand was a first aid manual entitled *The Red Cross First Aid* which went on to sell thousands of copies in over 20 different languages.

After an extremely successful career, Christopher decided to leave the company in 1987 and pursue other interests. The year after Christopher's departure, Peter launched the well-known *Eyewitness Guides* to fill the hole in the market for exciting non-fiction children's books. Famous for being a leading children's publisher, there are now 150 titles in this series and the series has sold over 50 million copies worldwide.

To new heights

In 1990, after a collaboration with Reader's Digest ended, DK approached Microsoft with the proposal of using DK's content and Microsoft's software to branch out into multimedia. Microsoft bought a 26% share in DK for £2.3m ($4m), and loaned the company £2m to set up DK Multimedia in 1991 and it soon launched its first CD-ROM, *Musical Instruments*. The multimedia strand of DK was to be significant in company's expansion. Although a highly competitive field, in 1996, the division contributed 12% (£21.2m, $31.5m) of DK's sales.

In 1992, DK went public, selling 19 million shares for £23.5m (Peter retained about 51% of the company).

During this time, DK was embarking on several new ventures, including DK Publishing inc, which established a publishing house in America. Instead of licensing book rights to other publishers, DK was now intent on becoming a publisher in its own right. After years of successfully 'packaging' books to the USA, in 1991, DK began publishing in America under its own name for the first time.

During the mid 1990s, DK acquired three publishers: Henderson Publishing, Hugo Language Books Ltd and Acacia, which enabled DK to buy into specialist areas of the publishing industry. By 1996, DK had sales of £174.4m ($279m) and in his shareholder statement, Peter announced that the publisher was 'poised to raise its profile to brand-name status'.

A RANGE OF DK'S HEALTH TITLES

A memorable decision

The original three Star Wars films are some of the most popular films ever released; as a result, demand for the 'prequels' was almost at fever pitch as the first film came close to being released. As usual for blockbuster films, companies were falling over themselves to sell licensed merchandise for the new film, including books. DK won the contract to produce official Star Wars books. Estimating sales for any new product is difficult; illustrated books tend to be printed in South-East Asia which means that it typically takes three to four months to receive the books after an order is placed. So for possibly the biggest commercial film release ever, DK wanted to make sure they didn't run out of stock; how many copies should they print? As has been well documented in the press, in 1999, anticipating storming sales, DK decided to print a colossal 13 million copies, but only sold around three million of these. Ten million unsold copies of an illustrated book would be an enormous problem for any publisher; it proved a major blow to DK. Subsequently, in March 2000 the company was acquired by Pearson for £311m ($463m) and now lives on as part of the Penguin Group umbrella. In the same year, Peter Kindersley retired after nearly 40 years in publishing, and now runs an organic farm in Berkshire.

Where are they now?

Under the stewardship of Andrew Welham, global managing director, and with the support of Penguin's sales and marketing divisions, DK moved on from the Star Wars debacle, and enjoyed success with new publications such as *Animal* and *The Ultimate Robot Kit.*

As well as building on the large backlist of reference titles, DK introduced a number of author-led books, including Bill Wyman's *Rolling With The Stones*, *Supersex* by Tracey Cox, and Monty Don's *The Complete Gardener.*

In July 2005 Gary June, an experienced publisher with strengths in sales, marketing and new business creation joined DK as CEO. DK continues to dominate the quality illustrated family reference and children's markets, and is still investing in big ambitious global projects like 600 page books on history and art. It now publishes in 44 languages, in 60 countries, and sells the world's bestselling travel guide series, *Eyewitness.* They are continuing to redefine children's reference with titles like *Pick Me Up*, a *New York Times* bestseller, and working with leading expert authors like BBC *Top Gear*'s Richard Hammond's *Car Science.*

DK is a global company, with offices around the world including those in the larger Penguin organisation and some that are standalone, like Germany and Canada. Innovation is still at the heart of what they do – selling content digitally across multiple platforms including mobile, ebooks and web – with recent deals for travel and medical content to Visa, MSN Latino, Net Trav and the Dutch government amongst others. The name DK has become synonymous with quality illustrated and reference publications across the globe as a result of their innovative and unerring vision for their products.

Lonely Planet

ONCE WHILE TRAVELLING

Founders: **Maureen and Tony Wheeler**

Age of founders at start: **22 and 26**

Background: **Secretary and student at the London Business School**

Year of foundation: **1972**

Business type: **Travel publishing**

Countries now trading in: **Worldwide**

Sales and Profit: **£23.1m ($40m) and £4.3m ($75m)**

HOW **THEY STARTED**

tarted by newlyweds Maureen and Tony Wheeler after an epic journey through Europe and Asia, Lonely Planet was one of a raft of independent publishers aimed at an emerging culture of student backpackers in the 1970s. Since then, the imprint has grown to become one of the two largest travel guide publishers in the world, publishing guides to almost everywhere in the world – including, controversially, Burma. However, the guides press on, and having recently been credited in *The Times* with 'single-handedly inventing the genre of the independent travel guide', Lonely Planet continue to produce travel guides and television programmes globally.

Starting out

As with many successful businesses, Maureen and Tony Wheeler stumbled into book publishing purely by accident. In fact, the idea came after their first journey together: having postponed a job at the Ford Motor Company after he graduated from the London Business School in 1972, Tony and his new wife, Maureen, decided they wanted one final taste of student freedom.

The pair set off on their adventure of a lifetime from Tony's parents' house in Berkshire in early 1972 on a trip which would take them through Europe, around Asia and down to Australia. Unlike today, at the time backpacking through Asia was almost unheard of.

'I don't think we knew anyone who had been to Asia,' says Tony in *Once While Travelling: The Lonely Planet Story* (Crimson Publishing 2008). 'Although I recall a Chrysler engineer once telling us that he had driven to the other side of Turkey in his flimsy Triumph Spitfire sports car.'

New beginnings

The pair arrived in Australia on a yacht in July 1972, where they quickly settled in, swiftly finding jobs and a small apartment in Sydney. Even during the first few months, Tony says they knew the year-long trip would be longer. 'Even now, almost 30 years later, I can recount day by day what we did during the last six months of 1972. How often in life is every day lit up so vividly?' he asks.

It was during this time that people started to ask them questions. 'Every time we went to a party or met people at a work function, questions would come up about our trip. How did we do it? How much did it cost? What's Bali like? Is Afghanistan dangerous?' Tony recounts. It wasn't long before they were writing the information down, and considering selling it. The only problem was finding a publisher – but Tony had a solution. 'We didn't need a publisher. I knew how to put a book together – we could publish it ourselves.'

TONY AND MAUREEN, ON EXMOUTH BEACH IN WESTERN AUSTRALIA, A FEW MOMENT AFTER THEY HAD ARRIVED IN THE COUNTY

'Even now, almost 30 years later, I can recount day by day what we did during the last six months of 1972. How often in life is every day lit up so vividly?'

Finding a press that would produce just 1,500 copies of a book proved complicated, but a coincidental meeting with Bill Dalton, whose travel imprint Moon Publications continues today, resulted in an introduction to David Bisset, who had a printing press in his basement.

So the pair's first guide, *Across Asia on the Cheap*, was nearly ready to go – but what to call their publishing house? Tony says the pair went through 'hundreds' of ideas, but it was when he got the lyrics wrong to the Matthew Moore song *Space Captain*, that they stumbled across the name. Tony recalls singing 'Once while travelling across the sky, this lonely planet caught my eye'. The lyric was actually *lovely* planet, but the slip-up stuck and Lonely Planet became the name of the Wheelers' new publishing house.

HOW **THEY** STARTED

Gearing up for success

Success came fairly fast for the first book. Having bound their own books, the Wheelers persuaded Angus & Robertson, the biggest bookshop in Sydney at the time, to take 50 copies, and then went to try and sell it to other bookshops. By the end of the day, they had sold several hundred copies – and gained press attention when one of their orders went to a bookshop owner whose girlfriend was a journalist for a paper in Sydney.

That first review quickly gained the couple the publicity they needed. 'A review of our book followed in another newspaper and then we were invited to appear on a breakfast-time television programme', says Tony. 'This was a useful first lesson for us about the power of publicity. Soon our book was not only on the shelves, but sitting by the cash register and in shop windows.'

Ten days after the first review was printed, the pair delivered their last copy of *Asia on the Cheap* to paying customers and ordered a 3,500-copy reprint. Lonely Planet was making its first tentative steps into the world.

Having made a relative success of their first book, the couple set their sights on South-East Asia as their next project. The book, *South-East Asia on a Shoestring*, would document the couple's year-long journey around the region on a 250cc Yamaha DT2 trail bike.

After they had completed their second book, the Wheelers were faced with a classic small-business dilemma: late payment. Money was tight, and a distributor in New Zealand still owed them a substantial amount of cash from their first book.

Alistair Taylor had sold 'lots' of books, but still hadn't paid up – and trying to resolve the issue was proving impossible, says Tony. 'Polite reminders had no effect and when we called in the lawyers they had no success either. Eventually, Alistair announced he simply had no money.' Instead of giving up the ghost, and in a classic 1970s-style hippie transaction that was archetypal of the unusual way the Wheelers were to do business subsequently, Taylor offered them a sort of exchange. 'Would we be interested, he asked, in some books he couldn't get rid of in New Zealand?'

So in May 1974 'our ship came in', as Tony puts it. The pair received 400 copies of a book on how to build a geodesic dome entitled *Great Circles*, and 300 copies of a book on Jimi Hendrix. They sold the lot. 'Months later, Melbourne record shops were still asking if I had any more Hendrix books', laughs Tony.

By the end of 1975, Lonely Planet were ready to print another 10,000 copies of *Across Asia*, as well as a 10,000-copy reprint of *South-East Asia*. Having been previously turned down for a loan, Tony's parents agreed to guarantee a £4,000 loan (about £25,000 or $47,000 today) as well as a bank overdraft. 'For years, this was the total extent of our bank borrowings', says Tony.

Growing pains

By 1979 the imprint had grown to such an extent that all pretence of being a home-based business was abandoned, and Lonely Planet moved to an office in Melbourne. At this point, the Wheelers felt the brand was beginning to build up steam.

It was during this period that they decided to take on someone new, and Jim Hart joined them from the 'sinking ship' of one of Australia's biggest independent publishers, Rigby Books. 'At some point in 1979 it was agreed that Jim would buy 25% of Lonely Planet publications, for a somewhat indeterminate figure to be paid at a somewhat indeterminate time in the future,' says Tony.

The main problem, he adds, was how much to pay Jim. At the time, while the business was turning over about £60,000 ($120,000), it was still plagued by financial worries. 'That was paying our bills, meeting the royalty payments to authors, covering salaries and supporting us quite nicely, and in the second half of 1979 our sales were running 100% higher, but paying for Jim as well was not going to be easy,' says Tony.

That problem was compounded when 'Jim came in to work one day complaining of double vision; he went to an optician, who sent him to a doctor, who sent him to a specialist. There were brain scans and then Jim was in hospital with a cerebral aneurysm, a swollen vein in the brain which could easily rupture and lead to a stroke or worse.' At the same time more problems arose following the birth of Tony and Maureen's daughter Tashi.

In early 1981 with Jim out of action and a 'new daughter who never slept,' Tony found himself not only with a double workload, but also taking on more and more projects to expand the company to the stage where it could support all of them. 'Lonely Planet was still teetering on the brink of disaster' he recalls. 'I was trying to be everywhere at once and as a result running myself ragged.'

'Fortunately things turned round with dramatic speed later that year when we published our first India guidebook,' Tony recalls. 'We'd almost bet the company on that single title, a much bigger and more complex guidebook than anything we'd published before. Fortunately India was a critical and popular success, selling far more copies than any of our earlier titles and at a much higher price.'

Back on the straight and narrow

The business pulled through, and by 1982 was ready to update its 'marginal' 192-page Australia guide to a 576-page epic. The book was released with the serendipitous timing that characterised many of Lonely Planet's releases: *Crocodile Dundee* was due to kick-start Australia's tourist industry shortly after the book's release, and as a result it went on to sell 60,000 copies.

It was around this time that Lonely Planet decided to make its first foray into the digital era, with the acquisition of computers. While the company's staff got used to

THE GROWING LONELY PLANET TEAM OUTSIDE THEIR OFFICE IN RICHMOND, MELBOURNE IN 1981. TONY IS KNEELING AT THE FRONT AND MAUREEN IS HOLDING THEIR BABY DAUGHTER TASHI.

the new additions, they caused some problems – not least that employee's jobs had to be rejigged to fit around them. 'Previously, there had been a neat division between editorial and design – the editors handled the words, the designers put them on the page in appropriate places,' says Tony. 'But suddenly all the decisions were being made by computers rather than people – and who oversaw the computers?'

Once the Wheelers were confident that their business could handle the implications of the new technology, they decided to set up a new office in the USA, and moved to San Francisco in 1984. 'Looking back, the decision to expand overseas by opening a sales and distribution office in the United States was either very brave or very foolhardy because at the time the Lonely Planet workforce was still less than a dozen people – not the sort of base from which to launch a multinational operation,' recalls Tony.

'Looking back, the decision to expand overseas by opening a sales and distribution office in the United States was either very brave or very foolhardy'

Foolhardy or otherwise, the Wheelers – now with a new addition, their son Kieran, who was just coming up to his first birthday – reasoned that until they had a US presence, they would never develop their market, and left Australia in 1984 to set up shop in Berkeley, California. 'Our US plan was simplicity itself: Maureen and I would go to San Francisco, open an office, find people to run it, return to Australia, and sell lots more books', divulges Tony.

Of course, this all proved to be easier said than done. Visa applications were the first obstacle: in the end, an American embassy official advised them, off the record, to go to the USA on a six-month tourist visa, rather than going the official route. 'Forget about doing it legally', she told Tony. 'We'll tie you up in red tape and never issue the visas.'

Sales didn't speed along as quickly as the pair hoped, and it soon became clear that they needed to do their own distribution. They took on Robert Sheldon, a 'character you don't easily forget' to take over the distribution side. 'It was no secret that his career had been, shall we say, colourful. I'm not quite sure to this day how Robert marched into Lonely Planet, but he was soon on the payroll as a part-time consultant', remembers Tony.

By early March 1985, sales from the US operation were slowly building but it was still, in the words of Tony, 'haemorrhaging money', and the family faced another problem: their visas were due to expire. 'We devised a simple way around this one-year limit: we'd leave the country for a couple of months, then come back and start again with another six-month stamp on our passports.'

Homeward bound

In July 1985, the Wheeler family returned to Australia, where they found their business transformed. The pair's partner, Jim Hart, had 'done a fine job keeping things not only going, but actually growing', and some angry words were exchanged when Tony 'thoughtlessly acted as though we were back in the driving seat', he says.

However, things quickly settled back down and, after sorting out some more glitches with the US operation, Tony decided he needed a 'travel fix' – and what better way to do that than by updating their India book?

India was an unusual trip for Tony: not only was he attacked by a particularly ferocious 'holy' cow, breaking two ribs in the process, it was also the first occasion on which he would hear tales of his own death – an event which for a spell regularly punctuated his travels.

'A group of us were sitting at our hotel's restaurant early one evening when a couple said a week earlier, in the south of India, they'd heard I'd been killed. I forget how I had met my end, I think it was in a train crash. We laughed it off, but a couple of weeks later, in a lakeside restaurant in Pushkar, another couple told me a similar story, except the nature of my death was completely different. Again I laughed it off, although hearing that you've died once is odd and hearing it twice is a truly remarkable coincidence.'

HOW **THEY** STARTED

Homeward bound

The following year the hard work breaking into the American market had paid off. 'The list had grown by a third, but our sales had grown by a 100% and for the first time we made a real, write-home-about-it profit,' explains Tony.

From £20,000 ($26,000) in 1984–1985, the business' profit had 'zoomed' to more than a quarter of a million the following year. There was no doubt that the publishing house had captured the imagination of travellers all over the world, and by 1991, the decision was taken to expand to Europe. In fact, notes Tony, 'we were in Europe, with an office, before we really got into Europe with our books.'

There was no doubt that the publishing house had captured the imagination of travellers all over the world

However, this would soon be rectified – the group had been thinking about doing guides to Europe since 1987, and in 1993 launched their first Europe series, with guides to Scandinavian, eastern, western, and Mediterranean Europe all hitting the shelves.

In fact, the launch of the European guidebooks went 'pretty much according to plan' – but while they sold as expected, they didn't set the world alight. This changed, though, on the release of their first edition of their Britain guide a couple of years later, when the *Sunday Times* ran a piece detailing all the criticisms the book made of the UK, 'from the Queen's bad taste in interior decoration to the shonky development of Land's End in Cornwall'.

The ensuing publicity came not only from the UK but also Australia, who suggested the Brits were so touchy because their colonial attitudes had never quite faded, and Canada, who were fascinated by the stand-off between the two countries. 'We had the pleasure of Germaine Greer postulating that perhaps the author of the Cardiff section had been laudatory about the city because he'd got laid there, but the author of the Coventry section – me – "certainly hadn't been successful". It's an achievement to have Germaine Greer commenting on your sex life,' laughs Tony.

Part of the reason for the imprint's move into Europe had been down to unwanted competition. Penguin Books had bought a controlling stake in Rough Guides, 'our main competitor in the British market now had a parent with very deep pockets,' recalls Tony. Penguin seemed to be targeting the brand by aggressively undercutting them: something needed to be done.

'We decided to hit Rough Guides head on. We ranked all their European books by sales and decided to produce a competing title for every one, starting at the top and working down.' The result was that by 2000, Lonely Planet had more titles on Europe than their competitor.

AN EMBLAZONED TAXI, TO CELEBRATE THE LAUNCH OF LONELY PLANET'S NEW LONDON GUIDEBOOK IN 1998

Turning a sow's ear into a silk purse

It was during this period that the brand reached the stage where, as Maureen puts it, 'business school students do a case study analysing your success.' One of the students, Steve Hibbard, suggested he join them for six months to work out how the business could become more efficient, and ended up staying with them for 10 years as their CEO.

While Steve was there, the imprint faced a mistake which could potentially destroy its reputation. Spelling mistakes plague almost every publishing house, but when the company found a spelling mistake on the cover of their *Western Europe* title, they were faced with a dilemma. 'We printed 40,000 copies of this bestselling 1,376-page work and then discovered that the spine proudly proclaimed it was not a guide to *Western Europe*, but to *Westen Europe*.'

A decision had to be made over whether to pulp the entire print run, put a sticker on covering up the mistake, or simply to admit to it. Lonely Planet went one better: they turned it into an advantage.

Tony came up with the idea of inserting a bookmark which featured an imaginary scene with two 'warehouse guys' debating the spelling of 'western'. 'Looks like somebody ****ed up,' says one. Below was another made-up scene, this time in a publishing meeting. 'We could just confess, put an errata slip in the book, make a bit of a joke about it,' suggests Steve, the CEO on the bookmark. The resulting publicity meant the book sold out at record speed. 'Some articles even suggested the book might become a collector's item,' says Tony.

It was perhaps this risk-taking attitude which allowed the brand became a pioneer of new technology. In October 1994, during a week of celebrations for its 21st birthday, Lonely Planet launched its first website. The site, launched a month earlier than Yahoo!, became one of the first to feature advertising on their site, and won its first 'Webby' award shortly thereafter.

Since then, technology has played an important part in the development of the brand. The site's Thorn Tree forum has become the first stop for travellers to find and share their knowledge. Tony even became one of the first bloggers, when he took a laptop on a journey around the USA, publishing an online diary as he went.

Technology has played an important part in the development of the brand

In 1992, the Wheelers were approached by Pilot Productions about producing a Lonely Planet TV series. Funding was obtained from various sources and the series launched on Channel 4. Although, in the words of Tony, 'it didn't make much money', the series, fronted by 'pint-sized, one-man energy source' Ian Wright (not the footballer), added yet more nouse to what was becoming an increasingly recognisable, multimedia brand.

Disaster strikes

The last months of 2001 saw Lonely Planet faced with what was arguably its most challenging period. There had been a period of turmoil when Jim Hart, their long-term partner, had left the company at the end of 1998, but things had calmed down when they gained the colourful Australian advertising entrepreneur John Singleton, or 'Singo' as he is known over there, as their new partner. And as the Twin Towers collapsed in clouds of dust and panic, the brand saw many of its hopes collapse with them.

September 11 brought fresh challenges: people were scared to fly and scared to leave the relative safety of their own regions. After September 11, the business was touch and go. Tourism had virtually ground to a halt, and Lonely Planet was forced to implement a raft of cost-cutting measures. 'On the morning of September 12, still early evening on September 11 in New York, we convened an emergency meeting,' remembers Tony. 'It was clear this was going to hit travel hard and we immediately looked for ways of cuttings costs. We dumped our free quarterly newsletter, delayed books to areas we felt were going to face tourist downturns or where we could reasonably put off a new edition, suspended new staff recruitment and began to look for other ways we could cut costs.'

As SARS, the Bali bombing, the Iraq invasion and the Madrid bombing all added up to wreak havoc for the brand, they decided their only option was to make significant staff cutbacks in the USA and UK, and later, in 2003, in their Australian office.

Five years on, and there have been even more changes to Lonely Planet: in October 2007, the Wheelers sold the brand to BBC Worldwide for a reported £40m ($74m), retaining a 25% stake. The move was a controversial one, and sparked debate among the licence-paying public, who wanted to know how the BBC would fund the private enterprise.

However, at the time, the pair said they felt they had made the right move. 'We're getting old', they told *The Times*. 'It allows us to secure the long-term future of our company within a globally recognised media group. We felt BBC Worldwide would provide a platform true to our vision and values, while allowing us to take the business to the next level', they said.

MAUREEN AND TONY, CELEBRATING LONELY PLANET'S 13TH BIRTHDAY WITH A REPRINT OF THEIR FIRST EVER BOOK, *SOUTH-EAST ASIA ON A SHOESTRING*, COURTESY OF FAIRFAXPHOTOS

Where are they now?

Even though the Wheelers have sold most of their stake in the company, Lonely Planet is still one of the world's most iconic travel publishers. Having laughed off a minor PR incident in early 2008 (a 'rogue' author claimed he had 'not even visited' one country he was writing about, saying he 'got the information from a chick' he was dating; in fact he had only been commissioned to write the history section of that book, a project which was never intended to be more than desk-based research), the brand has gone from strength to strength, publishing guides, phrasebooks and maps in eight languages, with 500 staff in three offices and more than 300 authors. The couple say the company is still driven by the philosophy of their first book, *Across Asia on the Cheap*: 'All you've got to do is decide to go and the hardest part is over. So go!'

Hilton Hotels

BE OUR GUEST

Founder: **Conrad Hilton**

Age of founder at start: **32**

Background: **Running a guest house, banking**

Year of foundation: **1919**

Business type: **Hotels and hospitality**

Country of foundation: **USA**

Countries now trading in: **74 countries and territories**

Turnover and profit: **Not available**

HOW **THEY** STARTED

Conrad Hilton purchased his first hotel in 1919 while on his way to buy a bank. Almost a century later the Hilton Hotels Corporation has grown to be synonymous with guest service and luxury hospitality, with more than 3,000 hotels and 500,000 rooms in 74 countries and territories worldwide. Hilton Hotels has been at the forefront of many of the innovations in the hospitality industry and still stays true to Conrad's philosophy that 'it has been, and continues to be, our responsibility to fill the earth with the light and warmth of hospitality'.

It all started with The Mobley ...

Conrad had a slender beginning in the hospitality industry, having run an inn in New Mexico with his father before he joined the army during the First World War. This inn came about after his father had the idea to see the family through financial difficulty by renting out the rooms of Conrad's seven brothers and sisters as they began to leave home.

In 1919 Conrad purchased The Mobley Hotel in Cisco, Texas. His original intention had been to buy a bank, and had already raised a share of the amount agreed with the bank manager himself, with friends chipping in the rest. The bank manager then upped his price, and Conrad walked away from the deal. That night, he went to get a room at The Mobley, but the hotel was full, as all rooms were sold in eight-hour shifts due to the need for accommodation during Texas' oil boom. Deciding that selling a hotel room three times a day seemed better than running a bank, Conrad sought out the owner and asked to buy the hotel. Wanting to get into the oil business himself, Mr Mobley accepted this offer, and Conrad used his already-raised capital of $35,000 (around $445,000 or £238,000 today) to buy The Mobley.

Deciding that selling a hotel room three times a day seemed better than running a bank, Conrad sought out the owner and asked to buy the hotel

Conrad quickly went about developing the hotel. After realising his clients' needs, he turned the unused restaurant into more bedrooms, and provided a fast-food service for the oil boomers, who needed to get back out to their oil fields quickly.

After just one year of owning The Mobley, Conrad had made his investment back and soon went on to expand his business. Conrad did not set out to create the global chain of hotels that exists today, but to expand his hotel chain in Texas, where he saw the opportunity for better quality hotels.

It was in 1923 that Conrad first developed the idea of the Minimax hotels. After observing hotel facilities throughout south-west USA and Texas in particular, he became convinced that the hotel world needed a strictly first-class chain of hotels; comfortable to the last degree and offering the public the maximum amount of service and satisfaction for the minimum cost.

With this business concept firmly settled in his mind he began in 1924 the building of the first hotel of the chain, the Hilton hotel of Dallas. The Dallas Hilton was opened in August of 1925, and was an immediate success. So much so that soon after, Conrad began his search for another location for a Hilton hotel.

West Texas was booming, Conrad was impressed with the city of Abilene and after a careful study of the situation, that city was selected for the site of the second Hilton of the blossoming system. The Hilton of Abilene, another modern hotel of 275 rooms was opened in September 1927. Conrad went on to buy the Melba Hotel in Fort Worth, Texas and the Waldorf in Dallas, Texas. He called these old hotels his 'dowagers', which he restored to show their true beauty.

Conrad's success came about as a result of his vision and innovation. It was reported that in the early days of building his business he chose to buy hotels which had individual reputations, and he claimed that 'I buy tradition and make the most of it'.

Depression hits

The Great Depression hit the hotel industry, and Conrad's hotel chain, hard. Conrad had planned to open a new hotel every year, however, shortly after announcing plans to build a $1.75m ($22.5m or £12m today) hotel in El Paso, the stock market crashed. He lost nearly everything: he was $500,000 in debt and was forced to give up many of his properties. Another setback occurred in the early years of the Depression when Conrad's dedication to the hotel business cost him his marriage. Conrad and Mary Hilton divorced in 1934.

After defaulting on his loans, his hotels were foreclosed on by the Moody family, owners of Galveston, Texas-based chain Moody Hotels. An agreement was made, and Hilton Hotels merged with Moody Hotels to form the National Hotel Company. Conrad was given the role of general portfolio manager and one-third ownership of NHC, but the tumultuous relationship with the Moodys resulted in the dissolution of the company in 1934. Conrad retained possession of three hotels from his original portfolio, in addition to a small cash settlement awarded in the dissolution. Conrad was able to once again focus on the development and growth of the Hilton Hotels in a strengthening economy.

In the Depression Conrad lost nearly everything he was $500,000 in debt and was forced to give up many of his properties

By 1937 Conrad had turned his luck around, paying off his debts through profits from oil leases that he had bought years ago, and purchasing eight more hotels.

A loyal group of managers had stuck by Conrad throughout the Depression, receiving bed and board in return for managing his properties and earning no salary for a much extended period of time. Pre and post-Depression, this allowed Conrad to seek out new investors, new properties and markets for expansion, while during the Depression, Conrad relied on his management team to maintain and uphold standards while challenging existing cost structures.

Comeback expansion

In 1938, Conrad started on the path of national and global expansion which would characterise the Hilton brand by purchasing his first hotel outside of Texas, the Francis Drake in San Francisco. This was not a conscious effort to expand nationally, but more a deal that could not be missed: the hotel had cost $4m to build, but was offered to Conrad for $275,000 ($4.3m or £2.3m today). This move also marked the beginning of the Hilton brand as a luxury hospitality group, with a focus on the business traveller.

The corporation expanded rapidly across the USA with hotels opening in New York City in 1943 and with the establishment of the corporate headquarters in Los Angeles. This expansion allowed Hilton Hotels to become the first coast-to-coast hotel chain in the USA, with Conrad's acquisition of the Roosevelt and The Plaza Hotels in New York City.

The purchase of the Francis Drake in San Francisco marked the beginning of the Hilton brand as a luxury hospitality group

In 1946 the Hilton Hotels Corporation was formed and in the subsequent year, Hilton Hotels became the first hotel company listed on the New York Stock Exchange, with Conrad having ownership of the majority of the shares, valued at more than $9m ($101m or £54m today).

In 1949, Conrad achieved one of his early dreams by purchasing 'the greatest of them all', the Waldorf=Astoria hotel in New York. Conrad had carried a picture of this hotel in his wallet and had finally realised his dream of owning it.

Hospitality goes global

1949 saw the expansion of Hilton Hotels into the international arena with the opening of the Caribe Hilton in Puerto Rico, where the Pina Colada cocktail was created. This

THE WALDORF=ASTORIA, 'THE GREATEST HOTEL OF THEM ALL', WAS PURCHASED BY CONRAD IN 1949.

expansion also signalled the formation of Hilton International, a separate corporation headed up by Conrad Hilton.

The first Hilton hotel opened in Europe in 1953 but Conrad also continued to expand his business back in the USA with the purchase of the Statler Hotel Company in 1954 for $111m ($914m or £489m today), at that time the most expensive real estate transaction in history. This acquisition increased the number of hotels Conrad owned to 28.

Other expansion milestones included the opening of Hilton's first hotel in Africa in 1959 and the building of the world's tallest hotel in London, the London Hilton on Park Lane in 1963. Conrad was quoted in 1966 as saying that he wanted to build hotels in every major city in the world.

In 1964 Hilton International split off from its parent company leaving Conrad Hilton as the president of the Hilton Hotels Corporation and its domestic properties in the USA. An agreement was made in which Hilton Hotels Corporation kept the exclusive right to use the Hilton name in the USA, while Hilton International had the right to the name throughout the rest of the world. Both the international and national company went on to make significant contributions in line with Conrad's initial vision and both were highly successful.

The end of an era

Barron Hilton took over as president and chief executive officer of the Hilton Hotels Corporation in February 1966. In 1967, Barron convinced his father, the biggest stockholder of Hilton International, to sell his Hilton shares to Trans World Airlines (TWA) in exchange for TWA's stock. Barron, an aviation enthusiast, thought the TWA stock would go up in value, but instead it plummeted. As a result, the International division was sold to TWA that same year.

Having continued to work six days a week throughout his career, Conrad Hilton died aged 91 in 1979. When Conrad died he had expanded his empire from The Mobley in Texas to 185 hotels in the USA and 75 others across the world.

Conrad reflected that 'to accomplish big things I am convinced you must first dream big dreams. True, it must be in line with progress, human and divine, or you are wasting your prayer. It has to be backed by work and faith, or it has no hands and feet. Maybe there's even an element of luck mixed in. But I am sure now that, without this master plan, you have nothing.'

Hilton International and global expansion

The Hilton International company survived a series of separate owners including TWA, UAL Corporation and was eventually sold to the British-based Ladbroke Group in 1987. In 1999 this group changed its name to the Hilton Group plc.

By 1987 the Hilton Group had established itself as the fastest growing hotel chain in the UK

After the split from its founder company, Hilton International continued its global expansion, opening hotels in Australia in 1969, Singapore in 1970 and Japan in 1984. The brand also furthered the luxury branding of its hotels by opening a safari lodge in Kenya in 1972. The Hilton name received even more global recognition when John Lennon and Yoko Ono held their famous 'bed-in for peace' in the Hilton Amsterdam in 1967.

By 1987 the Hilton Group had established itself as the fastest growing hotel chain in the UK and followed this success with further global expansion in 1988 with the opening of the first Hilton hotel in China in Shanghai.

In 1994 the company announced its vision for international expansion with plans to add another 40 hotels to its already impressive collection of over 200 hotels. The company decided to focus on developing first-class hotels based in city centres, international airports and luxury resorts.

Innovation continues

While Hilton International, and later the Hilton Group, expanded its prospects across the globe, the Hilton Hotels Corporation led the way in innovations in the hospitality industry, continuing Conrad Hilton's visionary plans.

Barron Hilton was a pioneer in financing and development for Hilton, as he established new deal structures that eventually became more popular within the hotel development industry. He was an innovator in many ways, from product and guest services, to operations, to financing and management of his hotels – he did not shy away from seemingly impossible deals, which perhaps his contemporaries and competitors would have.

Barron's strategy of managing hotels for third-party owners led to the rapid growth of his hotel empire.

In 1970, the Hilton Hotels Corporation became the first NYSE-listed company to enter the US domestic gaming market when it purchased the Las Vegas Hilton and Flamingo Hilton in Las Vegas for $112m.

Barron's strategy of managing hotels for third-party owners led to the rapid growth of his hotel empire

Hilton also launched a new chain, CrestHil by Hilton which was aimed exclusively at the suburban market in the USA. In time, CrestHil would form the foundation of what would become the Hilton Garden Inn chain of hotels.

HOW **THEY** STARTED

Hilton Hotel Corporation was also involved in many technological innovations in the industry, such as the introduction of HILTRON in 1977 and Hilton*Net in 1985, both systems providing revolutionary reservation and reporting synchronisation between hotels, sales offices and reservation centres. In 1995, the corporation led the way once more by launching its own internet site, a first for any major hotel chain. This allowed guests to make bookings 24 hours a day. Refusing to rest on its laurels, Hilton continued in its role as industry leader and innovator by securing a deal with American Express Financial Services to offer a no-fee hotel rewards credit card, the Hilton Optima Card, the first of its kind. This move echoed back to Conrad Hilton's decision to launch the Carte Blanche credit card back in the 1950s.

The Hilton Hotels Corporation also made its own expansion into the global market with the launch of the Conrad International Hotel chain in 1982. This was followed in 1996 by the global expansion plan which began the development of more than 200 Hilton Garden Inn properties, a brand which aims to provide comfortable accommodation to the mid-scale market segment. The corporation further expanded globally through its gaming links when it bought the Bally's Entertainment Corporation in 1996 making Hilton the largest casino gaming company in the world and allowing them to enter the highly lucrative market of Atlantic City. This move proved so successful that in 1998 the corporation created a separate company for its gaming business named Park Place Entertainment, ultimately becoming Caesar's Entertainment. This autonomous company took control of all Hilton, Flamingo and Bally branded hotel-casinos owned by the corporation.

Two companies, one brand

Since Hilton Hotels Corporation still owned exclusive rights to the Hilton name and brand there were some shared schemes with Hilton International, including many of the industry innovations made by the company. In addition to its sophisticated technological platforms, additional guest programmes such as the HHonors Reward Exchange further enhanced Hilton's ability to offer a seamless experience between Hilton and Hilton International properties. This programme became the first system in the world which allowed guests not only to collect loyalty points at Hilton hotels but also to exchange these points for air miles. Initially launched in 1987 in the USA by Hilton Hotels Corporation, HHonors would further solidify the value and power of the Hilton brand and cement its place as a leader in innovation.

In 1997, the Hilton Hotels Corporation and the Hilton Group plc made an alliance which brought the Hilton name back together for the first time in over 32 years and allowed the companies to operate under a united brand worldwide. This was followed in 1998 by the launch of a new logo and branding which unified the identity of both companies. The companies also began to make use of a central reservations system further aligning the two companies in the eyes of the consumer.

A MODERN HILTON HOTEL, IN MANCHESTER

HOW **THEY** STARTED

Spurred by a commitment to growth, in 1999, Hilton Hotels Corporation acquired Promus Hotel Corporation in a $3.7bn transaction expanding Hilton's portfolio to more than 1,800 hotels in all 50 states of the USA. Soon after Hilton's acquisition of Promus, Hilton announced the roll-out of Hilstar, the successor to the HILTRON reservations platform.

International meets innovation

After seven years of operating under this united front, in 2005 Hilton Hotels Corporation purchased the hotel interests of Hilton Group plc for $3.3bn (£1.8bn), reuniting the Hilton corporate entity Conrad Hilton had created in 1953 and allowing Hilton Hotels to become one of the fifth largest hotel operator in the world.

By merging the two companies, Hilton Hotels Corporation became geographically one of the world's most diverse hospitality groups. The company found itself in possession of nearly 2,800 hotels and 475,000 rooms in 80 countries. The Hilton brand now owned and operated under a range of trusted brands including Hilton, Waldorf=Astoria, Conrad, Doubletree, Embassy Suites, Hilton Garden Inn, Homewood Suites, Hampton Inn and Hilton Grand Vacations Club.

> *By merging the two companies, Hilton Hotels Corporation became geographically one of the worlds most diverse hospitality groups. The company found itself in possession of nearly 2,800 hotels and 475,000 rooms in 80 countries.*

Upon the completion of the acquisition in February 2006, Stephen Bollenbach (who became president and CEO in 1996) announced that 'this is one of the most noteworthy days in the history of our company, as Hilton is once again a global hotel company for the first time in over 40 years.'

Blackstone steps in

Following its move to become one of the most recognised and respected names in the hotel industry, the power of the newly reunited Hilton Hotels Corporation was clearly evident to consumers, but particularly recognised by leading investment firms. In July 2007 the Blackstone Group announced it would acquire HHC in an all-cash buyout valued at $26bn (£12.69bn) with Blackstone paying $47.50 per share for the Hilton Hotels Corporation. The Blackstone Group, who owns a vast portfolio of brand names across all industries, is an alternative asset manager and the world's largest private equity firm. This merger allowed the Blackstone Group to become the largest hotel owner in the world.

Following the announcement of the proposed merger, shares of the Hilton Hotels Corporation rose by 26% and on 24 October 2007 Hilton's stock ceased to trade on the New York Stock Exchange. With regards to the future of the company, the senior managing director of Blackstone, Jonathan Gray, announced that the company was 'committed to investing in the company and working with Hilton's outstanding owners and franchisees to continue to grow and enhance the business'. This focus on expansion echoes the rapid growth which characterised the company in its early days.

Where are they now?

In 2008 Hilton announced the appointment of a new senior leadership team in their bid to 'position Hilton as the premier global hospitality company'. This emphasis on the proposed growth of the company outlines the proposed future of the Hilton brand and everything it stands for.

Hilton also announced its commitment to global sustainability; with their presence in over 70 countries and serving over a quarter of a billion guests a year Hilton has announced they are in a powerful position to make an impact on the sustainability of global businesses.

The future for Hilton seems to be focused on continuing their commitment to global expansion and innovation. Despite the recent changes in the leadership and ownership of the Hilton organisation, these commitments to growth and innovation demonstrate the continuance of their corporate mission and legacy to 'become the first choice of the world's travellers' through Conrad's conviction to 'spread the light and warmth of hospitality'.

IKEA

A FURNISHINGS EMPIRE

Founder: Ingvar Kamprad

Age of founder at start: **17**

Background: **Child entrepreneur, selling matches**

Year of foundation: **1943**

Business type: **Furniture retailing**

Countries now trading in: **36**

Turnover: **£16.8bn ($30bn)**

HOW **THEY** STARTED

You've almost certainly got a pretty good sense of what IKEA is; you've probably been to one and spent hours assembling some of its flat-packed furniture. You might not know that this huge and successful business was set up by a highly impressive 17-year-old, or that his ethos has built a company culture so eccentric and passionate it's bordering on evangelical. Welcome to the world of IKEA.

Yet its beginnings were nothing if not humble. So, are you sitting comfortably? (IKEA chair optional).

Starting young

It was just a few years before the Great Depression of the 1930s which would so shape his life and business ethos. Ingvar Kamprad was born in the village of Agunnaryd in southern Sweden's Smaland, in 1926. Raised on a farm called Elmtaryd, at a time of great global economic uncertainty and lengthy soup kitchen lines, Ingvar quickly learned the value of thrift and displayed an extraordinarily early aptitude for entrepreneurship.

At just 5 years old, Ingvar bought matches in bulk and sold them from his bicycle at a profit. Quickly addicted to the thrill of selling, he expanded into ball-point and fountain pens, Christmas cards, fish, garden seeds and lingonberries (on your next visit to IKEA, you may want to check the food store for lingonberry jam).

'I suppose I was slightly peculiar in that I started tremendously early doing business deals. My aunt helped me buy the first hundred boxes of matches from the 88-ore bazaar in Stockholm in a large pack costing 88 ore . . . then I sold the boxes at two to three ore each, sometimes even five ore, so I was able to earn an ore or two in between. Talk about profit margins, but I still remember the lovely feeling. I can't have been more than five at the time' he recalls in *Leading by Design, the IKEA Story* (Bertil Torekull Harper Business 1999).

Still more startling is that Ingvar succeeded when faced with an unusually bleak family background: his beloved uncle Erich, his father's brother, committed suicide, as did his paternal grandfather; then there was the death of his 'heroine in silence', his mother from cancer at 53 and the implacable will of his paternal grandmother. Furthermore, Ingvar was dyslexic.

Commerce was, as Kamprad readily admits, in his blood. His mother came from a leading trading family in Almhult; her father and Kamprad's beloved grandfather, who would prove a pivotal influence, was Carl Bernard Nilsson, the owner of Almhult's largest country store.

According to Kamprad in *Leading by Design*, it was ' . . . a country store of the old kind with four or five assistants, the smell of herring and toffees and leather . . . Everything between heaven and earth could be bought there, even dynamite. Grandfather never made any demands on me, and sometimes I could spend whole days in the

THE FOUNDER OF IKEA, INGVAR KAMPRAD

shop . . . Unfortunately, he was just as kind in business life as he was in my invented world. He quite simply found it difficult to accept payment. CB Nilsson no longer exists as a business, but IKEA in a sense took over.'

IKEA begins

When he was 17, as a reward for success at school, his father gave Ingvar some money. Ingvar used this to found the business which became IKEA. The unique name comes from the initials of his own name, and those of places close to his heart: I for Ingvar, K for Kamprad, E for Elmtaryd and A for Agunnaryd.

So Ingvar founded IKEA Agunnaryd in 1943, aiming to sell goods by mail order.

He travelled across southern Sweden looking to find products to sell (not furniture to start with) and as he began advertising his goods for mail order, the seeds of the IKEA catalogue were sown. He continued to run the business while doing his national service, and received more mail than his own colonel.

1948 was a key year for the business – Ingvar began offering furniture, produced by local manufacturers near his home. He then produced a small brochure,

AN EARLY IKEA STORE SIGN

IKEA News, to advertise products including sofa beds and cut glass chandeliers. Because of his dyslexia, he found remembering the order numbers of goods problematic and decided that giving the items of furniture their own names would be much simpler. (Ah. So that explains the BILLY bookcase!) Beds, wardrobes and hall furniture are named for Norwegian place names; chairs and desks for men's names; materials and curtains for women's names and garden furniture for Swedish islands.

Because of his dyslexia, he found remembering the order numbers of goods problematic and decided that giving the items of furniture their own names would be much simpler

Business grew; so, later that year, Ingvar took on his first employee to help cope with the growth; two years on and the company had expanded to eight. In 1951 the company published the first IKEA catalogue and decided to focus entirely on furniture and home furnishing products. This worked well, and the business grew fast – by 1959, the company had 100 employees.

Ingvar explains in *Leading by Design* the decision to focus on furniture: 'So by chance the furniture trade – which I entered in an attempt to imitate competitors ... decided my destiny. No other event in life pleases me more than the fact that I ended up there. My interest at first was purely commercial: selling as much decent furniture as I could as cheaply as possible. Not until the first complaints started coming in did I realise that it was quality that was lacking. One day that would force me to draw certain conclusions and choose another way.'

A new direction

By the early 1950s, the mail order business was becoming very competitive, which was driving down prices which led in turn to poorer quality products – good for neither business owner nor customer. This proved the impetus for an innovative and logical change in the IKEA business – the decision to create a permanent, accessible space for customers to view the products before buying, unlike the mail order experience.

Ingvar opened IKEA's first store in Almhult, Sweden, in 1953. The essence of the IKEA experience was to provide a wide range of affordable, well-made goods for customers to see and touch for themselves in actual room settings.

'Mail order and furniture store in one. As far as I knew, that business idea had not been put into practice anywhere else. We were the first.' says Ingvar, justifiably proud of the achievement.

The impact was immediate and impressive. His decision to provide coffee and buns to the customers at the inaugural opening was also key; it formed the basis of today's popular IKEA in-store restaurants (the first of which opened in the Almhult IKEA store in 1960).

The essence of the IKEA experience was to provide a wide range of affordable, well-made goods for customers to see and touch for themselves in actual room settings

Another significant decision also came about due to the threat of competition: around 1965, when rivals were up in arms at the way IKEA was undercutting their prices, calling for suppliers to boycott IKEA, in a masterstroke, Ingvar turned this threat into an opportunity by starting to design their own furniture.

Revolutionary flat-packing

Their pioneering flat-packing concept was discovered in something of a eureka moment now turned company legend. Draughtsman Gillis Lundgren was having real trouble trying

THE EARLY FURNITURE IKEA OFFERED, IN A ROOM–STYLE SETTING

to fit a wooden table into a car for safe transportation. 'Oh God', he said resignedly, 'let's pull off the legs and put them underneath.'

While its not exactly up there with Einstein's theory of relatively, it developed into a pivotal selling point for IKEA: now that it develops and designs furniture so that it can be packed unassembled, it can pass the reduced costs of labour, shipping and storage on to the customer and as a result offer furniture at substantially lower prices than its competitors. As well as the financial side, the invention of flat-packs was beneficial to the environment, as more packs can fit into one lorry, meaning fewer trucks on the roads. IKEA's flat-pack design celebrated its 50th anniversary in 2006, and has been adopted by others in the furniture industry – this was truly a revolutionary invention.

Over the next few years, IKEA would expand internationally at a rapid pace. The flat-packing phenomenon meant its furniture could be shipped relatively cheaply; it involved customers in the value chain by enabling them to assemble their own furniture at home and its thrifty ethos brought cost savings. Crucially for its European expansion, those customers bought along similar lines. IKEA grew at almost the rate of a new country every year; Denmark in 1969, Switzerland in 1973, Germany in 1974, Australia in 1975, Canada in 1976, Austria in 1977 and the Netherlands in 1979. Its method was simple but strategic: IKEA would at first initiate and develop a relationship with a supplier in the target country; with the subsequent provision of legal, cultural, financial and political support and insight, this would ease the store's eventual launch. In 1965 IKEA opened its largest store at the time, in Stockholm, Sweden. 31,000 sq m in size, the ground-breaking store was modelled on the New York Guggenheim museum. Its opening became quite an event, attracting thousands of customers. Its tremendous success led to the opening of a self-serve warehouse – a relatively new concept for the furnishings industry and an important part of the IKEA ethos, allowing customers to serve themselves.

'Mail order and furniture store in one. As far as I knew, that business idea had not been put into practice anywhere else. We were the first.'

Business booms

The first IKEA store opened in Paris in 1981 and a year later, Ingvar decided to change the corporate structure of his business, forming the IKEA Group. This has enabled IKEA to stay private, which Ingvar feels has been critical to their growth by allowing them to make decisions much faster than he thinks a public company could have done.

Alongside the expansion came the development of several of the iconic IKEA furniture pieces, from the POEM (later POANG) armchair in 1976 to the BILLY bookcase in 1978, again reflecting Ingvar's unique take on memorable product names.

With the growth of the business came the almost evangelical belief that Ingvar held about its purpose in people's lives; so much so that he documented his vision of IKEA in *The Testament of a Furniture Dealer* in 1976, which was given to staff as their Christmas present that year, and is now reverently handed to every new member of staff when they join. Decrees to employees include the best way to make use of every 10-minute slot of their day: 'You can do so much in 10 minutes' time; 10 minutes, once gone, are gone for good. Divide your life into 10-minute units, and sacrifice as few of them as possible in meaningless activity.'

By 1984, the print run for the IKEA catalogue had skyrocketed to 45 million copies. Today it claims to have the world's largest print run of over 190 million and a product range of around 9,500.

A visit to IKEA is predictable. You set out with the aim of spending just £50 but exit, like a rabbit dazzled by the headlights, having spent £500 on bookcases, ice-cube trays and picture frames, helped along the way by the little IKEA pencils and order forms so helpfully provided.

HOW **THEY** STARTED

IKEA has worked hard to ensure its brand is associated, not just with easy-living and quality products at affordable prices, but with social, environmental and philanthropic activism. In the last 15 years, it has launched various social initiatives and partnered with Save the Children, UNICEF and with the WWF to promote responsible forestry, prevent illegal logging and reduce greenhouse gases.

In 1986, Ingvar retired to make way for new president and CEO, Anders Moberg who would remain in the role until 1999. One of the IKEA inner circle, Moberg had worked with Ingvar for 30 years; his reign saw an impressive continuation of IKEA's aggressive overseas expansion: the UK, Italy, Hungary, the Czech Republic, Poland, Spain and China. Moberg later left the business, making way for IKEA's current CEO, Anders Dahlvig.

IKEA has not been without controversy. In 1994 the Swedish newspaper *Expressen* revealed that Ingvar had enjoyed a close friendship with Per Engdahl, the openly pro-Nazi leader of a far right Swedish political movement; so close in fact, that Engdahl was invited to Ingvar's wedding to his first wife, Kerstin, in 1950. Ingvar admitted the friendship was a result of the 'sickness' of his youth. In a letter to employees entitled 'The Greatest Mistake of My Life' he asked forgiveness, explaining that it was a part of his past that he deeply regretted and had quit after a couple of Nazi-style meetings. He devoted two chapters to the transgressions in his 1998 book *The History of IKEA*. In an interview after its publication he asked for forgiveness – he'd said everything he could on the matter.

PART OF IKEA'S CURRENT RANGE, ÄDEL WHITE FAMILY KITCHEN

Where are they now?

From selling boxes of matches to family and neighbours, Ingvar Kamprad created a huge home furnishings empire, with 253 stores in 24 countries and a further 32 run by franchisees in 12 countries, selling a product range of about 9,500 items.

Over 560 million customers visit an IKEA store every year and the company has 1,380 suppliers in 54 countries.

More than 191 million copies of the door-stopping IKEA catalogue are printed in any given year; that's 56 editions and 27 languages (just how do you say flat-pack in Swedish?). According to Forbes magazine's list of the world's billionaires 2008, Ingvar Kamprad is the seventh richest man in the world with an estimated net worth of $31bn (£17bn).

Despite its size and success, IKEA continues to operate with a unique business culture, based on a number of passionate beliefs. One such belief is egalitarianism. IKEA regularly stages antibureaucracy weeks during which executives work on the shop floor or tend the registers. Even its CEO takes part, loading or unloading trucks in the IKEA warehouse.

More than just a business success story, Ingvar's IKEA is truly a phenomenon.

Apple

AN APPLE A DAY . . .

Founders: **Steve Jobs and Steve Wozniak**

Age of founders at start: **21 and 26**

Background: **Both computer technicians**

Year of foundation: **1976**

Business type: **Computers**

Countries now trading in: **Worldwide**

Turnover: **$7.51bn (£4bn)**

HOW **THEY** STARTED

When Bill Fernandez, a young computer enthusiast from the Santa Clara (later to be dubbed 'Silicon Valley'), introduced his friend Steve Jobs to Steve 'Woz' Wozniak in 1971, few would have predicted that the two would become the creators of one of the most innovative technology companies of the 20th, and, indeed, 21st century.

Starting out

After their first meeting Jobs quickly became fascinated with Wozniak, ostensibly because he soon realised Wozniak was the only person he'd met that knew more about electronics than he did, and soon realised the marketable value of his new friend's skills.

The pair's first commercial venture was selling 'Blue boxes'; electronic devices which could make free phone calls by imitating dial tone signals made by the phone company. The pair sold the boxes, which were based on an article in the October 1971 issue of *Esquire* magazine and designed by Wozniak, door-to-door in dorm rooms at Berkeley, splitting the profits. Rumour has it that during one display, Wozniak put on a fake German accent and posed as Henry Kissinger and dialled the Vatican, asking for the Pope. When the person on the other end of the line said the Pope was asleep but could be woken up, Wozniak hung up in fright.

Bountiful though the pair's first enterprise was, Wozniak, who was by now working for Hewlett-Packard, had always wanted to build his own computer. By early 1976, he had completed the design of his first machine, based on the MOS Technology 6502 microprocessor. The processor cost just $20 (about $100 or £51 today), which, compared to the $179 Intel 8080 chip which was increasing in popularity among computer hobbyists at the time, was a snip.

The completion of Wozniak's first computer design coincided with the 'golden era' of the Homebrew Computer Club, the hobbyists' group which was attended by personal computer masterminds such as Lee Felsenstein and Adam Osborne, both of whom played central roles in the development of the first mass-produced portable computer, the Osborne 1. Wozniak showed his design, which was little more than a circuit board at the time, off at the Homebrew Computer Club, where Jobs realised the pair could capitalise off it.

The computer, which could run BASIC, a sort of early programming language, and didn't have a monitor but was designed to be connected to the user's television instead, would eventually retail at around $650 (£325). Jobs persuaded Woz to pitch the idea of commercialising it to his boss at HP, who declined, telling him that the company 'didn't want to be in that sort of market', but Jobs was unperturbed, deciding the pair should go it alone.

To fund their initiative, each had to part with a treasured possession, and Jobs sold his red and white Volkswagen van for $1,500, while Wozniak sold his beloved HP 65 programmable calculator for $250. The company's name came shortly thereafter, when Jobs returned from a road trip with some friends announcing that a name had mysteriously popped into his head: Apple Computer.

The pair soon had one interested investor: Ron Wayne, a chief draftsman at video games company Atari, which Jobs worked for. However, Wayne pulled out two weeks later, citing Jobs' erratic personality as a reason.

Jobs returned from a road trip with some friends announcing that a name had mysteriously popped into his head: Apple Computer

Unworried by their latest let-down, Jobs began to peddle the 'Apple Computers' at the Homebrew Computer Club meeting, and got his first order from Paul Jay Terrell, who owned the Byte Shop Computer Store in Mountain View, California. The order was for 50 computers at $500 (£250) each, cash on delivery – the only hitch was that Terrell wanted the computers fully assembled, cases and all.

Once again, Jobs' unflappable nature shone through, and, having obtained a loan of $5,000 and persuaded suppliers to extend 30 days' credit on $15,000 worth of parts, Apple made its first delivery. This made an $8,000 profit (about $31,000 or £17,000 today) and eventually attracted the attention of Mike Markkula, a business angel who went on to invest $92,000 in the company. The early profit also helped the founders secure a $250,000 line of credit at the Bank of America for their new business.

Second helpings

During the early years, Jobs was very much driven by money, while Wozniak was fascinated by how far he could stretch the limits of technology. By the time the first Apple went on sale, he was already well on the way to completing a prototype for his second computer, and by July 1977 – just one month after the first model had gone on sale – Wozniak had completed the prototype for his second machine.

During the early years, Jobs was very much driven by money, while Wozniak was fascinated by how far he could stretch the limits of technology

HOW **THEY** STARTED

The catch with the second model, dubbed the Apple II, was that it cost hundreds of dollars to produce. To fund its production, Jobs attempted to sell the newly formed business to Commodore Business Machines, then an established manufacturer, but misjudged his negotiations and asked for too much money; Commodore turned the offer down. Fortunately for the business, Markkula stepped in, and the business filed for incorporation on 3 January 1977.

Product development for the Apple II was rapid. Jobs insisted on a sleek design for the computer, which resulted in a professionally designed case which he said would be more attractive to customers, and engaged the services of Regis McKenna, who designed the now-familiar logo. The logo featured an apple with a bite taken out of it – for which there was no better reason than it made the logo look more like an apple, and less like a cherry tomato. The logo's horizontal stripes, there to pay tribute to the machine's 'impressive' colour capabilities, would have been easier to produce if they had had black lines between them. The business' CEO at the time, Michael Scott, called the image 'the most expensive bloody logo ever designed'.

The computer went on sale in March 1977 at around $1,300 ($4,680 or £2,510 today), and was an overnight hit. Computer enthusiasts from across the USA were seduced by the machine's attractive casing, built-in keyboard and colour graphics capabilities. An ad campaign at the time promoted it as a machine for 'all the family', allowing you to balance books, play games and even learn arithmetic.

In 1978, a year after the computer launched, Apple released two products which catapulted the then still fledgling business into the electronics big leagues. The first was the Disk II drive, which allowed users to store more data than any other microcomputer on the market, and the second was a piece of software called VisiCalc.

VisiCalc, originally known as Calculedger, was the first piece of software to introduce home computer users to the idea of an electronic spreadsheet. The software, developed by two students from Harvard and MIT, sold 200,000 copies in its first year, and the Apple II saw a significant boost in sales when consumers started buying the hardware just so they could run VisiCalc.

Highs and lows

The emerging market for personal computers at this time was full of companies starting out; some achieved nothing at all, others achieved prominence for a while before crashing, while just a few made it through successfully. 1978 and 1979 saw the beginning of three major projects, two of which would see Apple itself come close to failure. In 1978, the company announced the Apple III, a machine which was supposed to mark Apple's foray into new technologies, but ultimately left their reputation in tatters.

1979 also saw Steve Jobs' first visit to Xerox's Palo Alto Research Center (PARC). The aim of the centre was to develop new technology without having to worry about the practicalities of funding.

On a visit to PARC, Jobs, along with Apple employee Jef Raskin, came across an early mouse-driven computer with a 'point and click' operating system. Jobs was tremendously excited by the concept, calling it 'revolutionary', and demanded the team which was developing Lisa, Apple's second technological failure, concentrate on developing a similar interface.

The third project on the cards at Apple was called the Macintosh. Having been booted off both the Lisa and the Apple III projects by disgruntled developers tired of having their decisions made for them, in 1980, Jobs took control of the Mac project, much to the consternation of the person in charge at the time, Jef Raskin.

Raskin and Jobs clashed, but Jobs' elevated status in the company gave him the freedom to make the decisions, and the project quickly took on an air of anarchy. The team working on the project were taken out of Apple's main office and moved to 'Texaco Towers', where a pirate flag was hoisted over the building. In fact, Jobs liked to refer to the Mac team as 'his band of pirates', and began to steal new ideas and innovations from the Lisa project. As a result, when the Mac launched in 1984, it was more compact and cheaper than the Lisa, but with the same technology.

With Jobs' takeover of the project, the goalposts for the Mac were rapidly being changed. At the beginning of the project, Raskin had outlined plans for a cheap, light, user-friendly machine, but as Jobs added new features to the plans, Raskin's vision was being destroyed. In 1982, Raskin resigned, leaving Jobs to oversee the entire project. As the machine's launch date approached, engineers were forced to put in longer and longer hours – eventually, the workers had a t-shirt printed which proclaimed: '90 HRS/WK AND LOVING IT'.

In November 1983, Super Bowl viewers were given their first glimpse of the hype which would surround the Apple Macintosh for years to come. As a melancholy onscreen voice told the viewers 'Why 1984 won't be like *1984*', a generation of consumers' computing habits would be determined.

Rotten apples

The Mac launched successfully in 1984, and inspired loyalty and admiration bordering on the obsessive among its fans, who loved how easy it was to use. The personal computing world was growing very rapidly, with a number of other competitors offering alternative computers; the main competition at this time was IBM with its own personal computer, and a slew of other manufacturers who made versions of it, all running an operating system made by Microsoft. And as if competitive threats were not enough of a challenge, although sales of the Mac rose steadily the internal workings of the business were not going as smoothly.

The Mac launched successfully in 1984, and inspired loyalty and admiration bordering on the obsessive among its fans, who loved how easy it was to use

After the company's initial public offering (IPO) in 1980, rifts had begun to appear between its co-founders. While Jobs was content to watch some of Apple's most influential employees, many of whom were still on temporary or freelance contracts and therefore not offered stock options, fall by the wayside Wozniak believed they should be rewarded for their work. As a result, he gave many of his shares away to those who he felt were 'deserving' of them, telling friends he already had enough money.

By 1981, after the failure of the Apple III project, the business was forced to lay off 40 of its employees. Wozniak took a leave of absence after a plane crash left him with serious injuries and forced him to reassess his options. He decided corporate politics weren't for him and went on to start work on other projects – most notably a series of music festivals which left him significantly out of pocket, and ultimately he turned to teaching. Wozniak retained a nominal salary, and while he returned to Apple in 1983 to do product development, it was as an engineer, rather than in an executive role.

After Wozniak's and, later on, Raskin's departures, the board of directors became tired of Jobs' arrogant leadership style and erratic behaviour, and forced him to resign. Jobs was heartbroken, but quickly recovered and started an education software business, NeXT, along with several senior members of Apple staff. When Apple bought that, he sauntered off to Lucasfilm, which was selling off its computer animation division, Pixar.

If the years after Jobs' resignation were anything to go by, Apple was in trouble. While the Mac continued to sell steadily, Microsoft launched its own operating system, Windows, which looked suspiciously like Apple's own OS. Apple attempted to sue the company, but made an out-of-court settlement when it realised Microsoft's CEO, Bill Gates, had been part of the development team of one of Apple's original operating systems. During this development, Gates had managed to pen an agreement with the company which included a loophole which allowed him to write an operating system which competed with Apple's.

In 1995, Microsoft launched Windows 95, which went on to sell three million copies in its first five weeks – compared to the 4.5 million Macs which Apple sold that year. The combination of more software being available for the IBM compatibles, as they were then known, and Apple's more expensive pricing meant that despite its technical superiority, Apple's market share fell steadily. When, during 1996, the business lost $740m (£500m), and Apple's new chairman, Gil Amelio, was embarrassed into resigning, it was clear something needed to be done or Apple would be in serious trouble. At one point Microsoft even bought a stake in the company in order to raise money to keep it going, citing its wish to retain its sales of Microsoft's software products such as Office for Mac computers.

Bouncing back

In 1996, the decision was made to put Steve Jobs back in the driving seat, initially as interim CEO. Having spent the intervening years running NeXT and Pixar, Jobs had calmed down, retaining all his passion for the business but now without his volatility.

Jobs immediately streamlined the company, shutting down a number of unprofitable projects which were sapping money. Terrorised employees voiced their fears of meeting Jobs in the elevator, but the reality was that Apple was on the brink of bankruptcy, and Jobs was doing everything in his power to bring it back.

Most notably, Jobs recruited London-based product designer Jonathan Ive to completely overhaul the design of the Mac. Jobs, whose first stipulations for the Apple II were that it should be aesthetically pleasing, was going back to his original instincts.

The result of the Ive-Apple partnership were the simple, brightly coloured, elegant, and friendly iMacs. At the time, these computers were a revolution – suddenly, consumers were proudly displaying their computers as a design feature in their homes, rather than having them hidden away in a study or an attic. Many people who had been staunch Windows supporters were converted to the Mac, and for the first time the similarities between Windows and the Mac OS were working against Gates – those who had become accustomed to Windows could very easily learn to use the Mac OS, meaning people had no trouble switching between the two.

Simple, brightly coloured, elegant, and friendly iMacs. . . at the time, these computers were a revolution

This proved the impetus for a new wave of products which were as cool to look at as they were easy to use. This boosted both Apple's market share and its profitability dramatically, turning around the fortunes of the company, although by then there were too many computers in the world running Windows to threaten Microsoft's dominance.

The next stage in Apple's continuing evolution came in 2001, when Apple launched the iPod. This literally revolutionised the music industry by providing a sleek, attractive device

HOW **THEY STARTED**

which was easy and even fun to use while letting people listen to their own music from electronic files (called MP3 files) rather than needing a CD or tape. Initially picked up by early adopters, the sales of iPod really exploded when Apple launched iTunes in 2003. This was a website which enabled people to download music onto their iPod from the internet, and crucially let them buy songs one at a time, instead of needing to buy entire albums. iTunes was easy to use, and people loved creating their own playlists where they could choose which track played when, rather than listen to every song on a CD in order as they had had to before. In June 2008, Apple announced that over five billion songs had been purchased and download from iTunes.

Jobs had done it again, placing Apple at the heart of a new consumer revolution. In fact, Jobs has been the business' saviour, with sales and profits rising once again.

Where are they now?

Despite the recurrent success of Apple, Jobs is far from through yet. Apple's most recent major launch, the iPhone, has revolutionised the style and functionality of yet another device, the mobile phone, and is selling extraordinarily well today. Unsurprisingly, Apple have more innovations planned for this, too.

Since 2003, Apple has been seducing consumers by putting brand new innovations in smaller and smaller packages. While computers continue to play an important role in the brand's portfolio (just ask any designer!), Apple is continuing to invest heavily in product development across all its product categories.

Jobs continues to play an integral role in the business, appearing at various conferences and MacWorld Expos to rapturous applause from his audiences. With the current board of directors including former US vice president Al Gore, and Google CEO Eric Schmidt, Apple looks set to be at the cutting edge of technology for a long time to come.

BlackBerry

(RESEARCH IN MOTION)

WIRELESS SUCCESS

Founders: Mike Lazaridis and Doug Fregin

Age of founders at start: 23

Background: Both engineering students

Year of foundation: 1984

Business type: Mobile communications

Countries now trading in: 140

Profit: £3bn ($6bn) (2007)

HOW **THEY** STARTED

Mike Lazaridis is every inch the inventor. Since co-founding Research in Motion, which is said to be the most profitable device maker in history, he has earned a reputation for being a true visionary of mobile communications – with good reason. This is the man who was studying wireless technology in the late 1980s before most people even had a home PC. The primary fruit of this research, the BlackBerry device, now enables millions of users around the world to check, send and receive emails while on the move. At the age of 46, he's now heading up one of the most successful and pioneering technology businesses in the world.

The early days

There were signs of Mike's inventive talents long before the world started to hear about them. The man who helped develop the world's first reliable portable email device made a record player out of Lego at the tender age of four. By 12, his fascination with engineering and the way things work became clear when he was awarded a prize at his local public library in Windsor, Canada, for reading every single science book on its shelves.

As a teenager, Mike is remembered by his peers, perhaps unsurprisingly, for having a seemingly endless bank of new ideas and inventions. In 1984, while studying electrical engineering at the University of Waterloo, he set up a company with childhood friend Doug Fregin to develop some of them. This company was backed by a New Ventures Loan from the government of Ontario, and by Mike's parents. Research in Motion (RIM) was born.

Founded as an electronics and computer science business, RIM caught a lot of people's attention and Mike, certain of its potential and desperate to devote all his time and energy to it, dropped out of university just a month before graduating to work on the business full-time. It was around this time that RIM won a major $600,000 contract with General Motors, one of the largest car companies in the world, to create an electronic display system. The creation of user-friendly electronic displays has since proved to be a particular strength for Mike, with the BlackBerry.

RIM was the first wireless data technology developer in North America

After the first big project with General Motors, a series of successive contracts generated revenue for RIM, and by the late 1980s sales had hit around $1m and the company had grown to employing 12 people. In 1987, a contract with Rogers Cantel Mobile Communications Inc, a mobile phone and pager operator, marked the beginning of its journey into wireless communications. RIM was the first wireless data technology developer in North America. Tasked with researching digital wireless devices, RIM developed a wireless radio modem, which was later used in products such as computers and vending machines and for business communications such as credit card transactions.

Funding growth

Throughout the 1990s, RIM focused its energy on the challenge of making mobile wireless emailing a reality. The company began working with Ericsson to enable its wireless data network to support two-way paging and wireless email, as part of a three-way partnership with Anterior Technology. In 1992, Mike hired James Balsillie to develop and run the business, freeing him up to focus on what he does best – engineering. Harvard MBA graduate James soon became RIM's chairman and

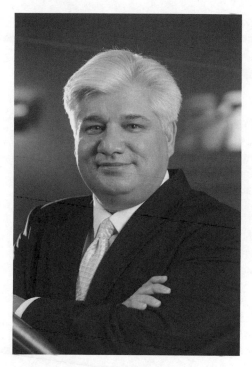

CO-FOUNDER OF RIM, MIKE LAZARIDIS, IS NOW PRESIDENT AND CO-CEO

co-chief executive.

James invested $250,000 (which is £120,000 or $212,500 today) into the business himself, and later helped secure $2m (which is £960,000 or $1.7m today) from COM DEV, a technology firm in Waterloo, Ontario, central Canada. The company also received $100,000 from the University of Waterloo's Industrial Research Assistance Program in 1994. Further research and development was later funded by venture capitalists, who invested in the company in 1995. In the first round of venture capital funding, Working Ventures Canadian Fund Inc made a $5m (which is £2.3m or $3.6m today) investment, which was used to complete the development of RIM's wireless hardware and software. During this time, RIM also received substantial investment in the form of loans and grants from the Canadian government.

In 1996, RIM developed a plug-in card for computer-enabled wireless email, and by the following year, the company had created a relatively small, handheld device that enabled two-way messaging via a pager for the first time (using BellSouth's wireless data network). Named the Inter@ctive pager, it was soon snapped up by companies such as IBM and Panasonic who distributed the devices to their field staff.

Realising the potential of their wireless email technology, but knowing just how much money it would take to pursue these opportunities, James and Mike knew they needed a substantial additional amount of capital. So RIM decided to go public. The company raised

$115m when it listed on the Toronto Stock Exchange in 1997, a further $250m when it floated on Nasdaq in 1999, and hot on its heels another $900m from a share issue in November 2000.

The birth of a phenomenon

The first BlackBerry was launched in 1999. This device made it possible for users to access their corporate email accounts (from a Microsoft exchange server) on the move. Its 'always-on' technology was an instant hit with customers, who were alerted when they received a new email and didn't have to go in and retrieve it. It cost $399, with a monthly subscription charge of $40. By 2000, it had already been named Product of the Year by *InfoWorld*.

The product was a commercial triumph. In 1999, sales of the BlackBerry more than doubled RIM's revenue to $47.5m, while net income (profit) rose to $6.8m. Central to BlackBerry's success was RIM's partnerships with the big internet service providers (ISPs) and telecommunications companies, and later, the mobile phone networks, to allow them to offer BlackBerry devices and tariffs. By the end of 1999, several major ISPs had already signed up to offer BlackBerry's services to their customers, including US RGN Corp and GoAmerica Communications Corp. Overseas, TelCel Cellular was offering two-way messaging through RIM's interactive pager across Latin America.

> *By 2000, the BlackBerry had already been named Product of the Year by InfoWorld. The product was a commercial triumph.*

RIM also negotiated distribution agreements with huge computer companies such as Dell and Compaq, whereby the computer companies' sales staff would sell the BlackBerry to their large corporate clients. As well as growing sales and profits quickly, this also helped raise the profile of BlackBerry. As early as the first year after its release, the devices started to crop up in business meetings, especially those featuring investment bankers and venture capitalists who thrive on being as up to date as possible. As a result, sales of BlackBerry devices took off in the US corporate market. In 2000, Nortel, the Canadian telecommunications company, invested $25m into RIM as part of a joint marketing and product development agreement with a view to extending BlackBerry's global reach. By the end of this year, revenue had grown to $85m, with a net income of $10.2m.

RIM were far from alone in their development of devices to access email remotely. Indeed, by the late 1990s email had become so central to most people's work in the development world that remote access to email was clearly going to be an enormous market. The first company to crack it would surely make billions in profit. Unsurprisingly there was lots of competition, from Microsoft and businesses such as Palm Inc, who had done so well with their personal digital assistant featuring a pen rather than a keyboard. BlackBerry took off because it came up with a way for people to access their email easily and fast on a small device. Systems such as Windows work very well but are very large, which makes them relatively slow on small computers. RIM's genius was to work well with Windows, but to use its own operating system which could be optimised for small devices and therefore worked far faster than Microsoft's equivalent.

Within minutes of having their BlackBerry set up, people were comfortable using them, unlike most other competitive devices trying to do the same thing

In addition to this BlackBerry did two other things which were unconventional but worked brilliantly. The first was to offer a 'Qwerty' keyboard that was large enough to be easy to use. The second was to use a 'flywheel' to move between emails and around the screen. This worked extremely fast, and people learned how to use it in literally a few seconds. Within minutes of having their BlackBerry set up, people were comfortable using them, unlike most other competitive devices trying to do the same thing.

Expanding overseas

By 2001, the BlackBerry, which now had its signature thumb-controlled keyboard, was beginning to make an impression on the European market. Agreements with telecommunications companies such as BT Cellnet, Digifone and Telfort Mobiel meant BlackBerry devices became available in the UK, Ireland and the Netherlands respectively. Meanwhile, expansion in the home market continued at a fast pace, helped along by more distribution agreements with the likes of

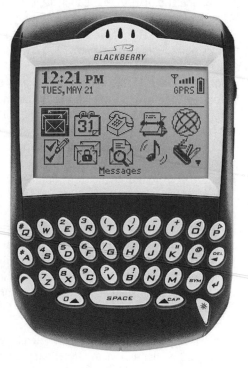

AN EARLY MODEL – THE BLACKBERRY 6210

HOW **THEY** STARTED

RIM'S HEAD OFFICE IN WATERLOO, ONTARIO CANADA

IBM. By the end of 2001, more than 12,000 organisations in North America were using BlackBerry devices.

By this point, RIM had sold over 200,000 devices and had forged a partnership with AOL to provide its email service through its handheld devices. While Palm Inc's range of PDAs were the biggest sellers in the overall market, the BlackBerry was fast becoming the device of the choice for business people who needed fast and reliable access to their corporate emails. But the early noughties brought stiff competition, not least the introduction of Nokia's SMS service. To remain competitive, in 2002, RIM began enabling third-party developers and manufacturers to enhance their products and services with wireless communications. It also began licensing its keyboard technology (which was uniquely controlled by a user's thumb) to its rivals Palm and Handspring.

A decision to partner with Hutchinson, one of Australia's biggest media technology companies who operate the mobile phone brand 3G, spelt the arrival of the BlackBerry 'down under'. Hutchinson Telecoms offers an industry-leading international roaming service which operates in over 149 countries. In 2001, Hutchinson was beginning to expand outside its native Australia, and promoted the BlackBerry device heavily throughout Asia and the Antipodes.

BlackBerry's launch in the European markets was helped by its development in 2002 of the 5810 model that incorporated mobile phone functions. In the UK, this led to a huge deal with Vodafone, and a similar agreement followed with Deutsche Telekom in

Germany. Over the following months, BlackBerry was launched in France, Italy, Spain and Switzerland. However, by 2002, RIM made net losses amounting to $28.3m as a result of the mounting costs of product development and international expansion. The company therefore made the decision to cut 10% of its staff.

By 2004, the company was back on course, and there were now 1.7 million BlackBerry subscribers worldwide. However, with 82% of these still based in North America, the company took steps to ramp up its international expansion plans. Europe was a particular focus, and in 2004, RIM had secured deals with most of the major European networks, including Orange and BT, which led to sales in this region doubling. Key to this success was the fact that BlackBerry sales staff were giving free trials to companies who wanted to give the devices to their workers. Around 90% of these ended up as paying customers.

Also in this year, RIM released a new version of its email server to support Chinese and Arabic alphabets and by 2005, Hutchinson's Hong Kong branch had partnered with language support company Onset to introduce Japanese and Korean language support functions for BlackBerry to users in Hong Kong and Macau. This partnership ensured BlackBerry could make significant headway into Japan and Korea.

Cracking the mass market

Throughout its history, RIM has continually raised its game when it comes to product development and has remained a true pioneer in the design, manufacture and marketing of mobile communications tools, winning numerous awards for product innovation.

While the BlackBerry was an instant hit with executives and fast-paced business people, the company has now adapted the model, with video cameras and music players, to draw in more retail customers. The BlackBerry Pearl 8100 was introduced in 2006 and helped shed BlackBerry's heavily corporate image. It's now quite common to see people playing games on BlackBerry devices on trains and planes.

The company has now adapted the model, with video cameras and music players, to draw in more retail customers

RIM has worked hard to make its email portals as secure as possible. Since becoming the first product to offer dependable mobile email in 1997, the brand has become synonymous with data security and is used by many customers who are sending sensitive, 'for your eyes only' material, be that A-listers or government bodies. The company has also faced several legal battles to protect its multi award-winning patented technology (serial inventor Mike holds more than 30 patents) from being used by competitors.

BlackBerry devices are now used all over the world and the company has offices in North America, Europe and Asia Pacific. The devices, which run on pretty much any network, have become so successful that many users (typically senior executives of large companies and business owners) now wonder how they ever lived without them. Unofficially dubbed the 'crackberry', their addictive quality has been widely reported. The option to receive an alert whenever a new email is received leaves many business people unable to resist the temptation to check out the latest addition to their inbox, no matter where they are or what the time is.

A BLACKBERRY PEARL 8100; THE PEARL SERIES HAS HELPED RIM CRACK THE CONSUMER MARKET

Where are they now?

In 2007, RIM was named one of Canada's Top 100 Employers, as published in *Maclean's*, Canada's leading business magazine, and was the only wireless technology company on the list. Meanwhile, the BlackBerry has continued to sweep the board in technology awards and league tables. These days, as well as incorporating a mobile phone, the devices feature a personal information manager including contacts, calendar, tasks and memo functionality, which can synchronise with the user's desktop. Users can also use a BlackBerry to access the internet and internet-based applications, while other companies have created applications that allow access to data from customer relationship manager (CRM) systems.

Last year, RIM was valued at $26bn, while Mike was estimated to be worth around $2bn. As co-chief executive, Mike is still heavily involved in the business he co-founded, where he is responsible for product strategy, research and development, product development and manufacturing.

BlackBerry, now available in over 140 countries, plans to expand further into Russia, Latin America, China and South-East Asia. More than seven million people around the world, primarily senior executives and business owners, use a BlackBerry to send and receive emails on the move. As the trend for flexible working increases, so the growth in the market for mobile devices shows no signs of abating. In the UK in particular, skills shortages have been well documented and employers are increasingly allowing staff to work more flexibly as a means of recruiting and retaining top talent, while legislative changes are gradually giving more and more workers the right to request this. Mobile technology has made this possible.

At the moment, BlackBerry holds around a 70% share of the market. Through partnering with some of the world's leading mobile phone producers, including Sony Ericsson, to help them develop their ranges of smart phones, it has maintained a strong position in this space, although a key partnership with Nokia recently fell through when the company decided they wanted to move forwards alone. RIM's future seems bright, as the market for this type of communication globally is sure to grow very significantly. As the prevalence of mobile working increases it is likely that more and more employees as well as decision-makers will start to get in on the emailing-on-the-go action. Last year, an article in the *Guardian* reported that just 1.2% of the 600–700 million corporate email accounts had been mobilised, which shows there is still scope for enormous growth.

Nintendo

REACHING THE TOP OF YOUR GAME

Founder: **Hiroshi Yamauchi**

Age of founder at start: **21**

Background: **University student**

Year of foundation: **1949**

Business type: **Computer games**

Countries now trading in: **Worldwide**

Net income: **£1.25bn ($2.5bn)**

HOW **THEY** STARTED

S ome years ago there was dismay in America when researchers uncovered the fact that Ronald MacDonald was better known among children than the US president. So imagine their shock when, during the early 1990s, it was found that home-grown cartoon characters such as Mickey Mouse had been surpassed by Super Mario, a foreign creation. The Japanese-made hero had become a part of children's lives across the world. And for the games maker Nintendo, the cheeky plumber with the moustache was to help make them one of the dominant forces in computer gaming. Today Nintendo is a £1.25bn business, rivalling Sony and some way ahead of Microsoft in this rapidly innovating business. Others, such as Atari and Sega, have fallen behind, unable to match the pace of innovation which the company has set.

A family affair

The company that we know and love today is largely the result of the vision and efforts of a man called Hiroshi Yamauchi. He inherited a very small family business which made playing cards from his grandfather in 1949 when he was just 21 years old. He was still at university when he was offered the chance to become the next president of the company and was unsure whether or not to take it. But after his grandfather agreed to his stipulations he dropped his studies and took over the helm. His family had produced playing cards for decades and had distribution outlets across Japan. However Hiroshi was keen that the company, then known as Yamauchi-Nintendo, was to have a bigger future. From day one he showed that he was going to run his company with a single mindedness and determination which often struck fear into those around him. Insisting that he be the only family member in the business, he had his grandfather fire his cousin before he assumed the role of president. He then began a major shake-up of the business: moving production, firing the managers that his grandfather had appointed and revamping the product range. Hiroshi was determined that no one would question his authority and long-standing employees soon learned where the power lay.

From day one Hiroshi showed that he was going to run his company with a single mindedness and determination

Following travels in the USA, Hiroshi 's Nintendo produced the first plastic coated playing cards in Japan. Then, in 1959, he made a deal with Walt Disney to produce cards featuring Disney characters on the backs, and sold over 600,000 packs. But despite this success Hiroshi was still not contented and sought out new ideas. While travelling in America he was shocked to find how small card manufacturers were there, which he saw as the writing on the wall for his own company. He listed the business on the Osaka and Kyoto stock exchanges and used the money raised to launch new products. For a brief period he stepped outside of games and tried an instant rice product, a 'love hotel' and a taxi service with mixed results. However, he soon tired of these and realised that his strengths lay in his strong presence in the toy shops which he had expanded into with the plastic coated cards. In 1969 he renamed the company Nintendo Games, the company that would ultimately lead to him to global success.

Fun and games

Hiroshi hired many engineers over the coming years and although he didn't possess any of their skills he had great success in motivating them to come up with countless innovations. He created competition among his inventors, but was also able to foster collaboration. Everybody wanted to please the boss and Hiroshi dished out praise and scorn in equal measure. Crucially he had a real knack of knowing when a product would sell and when it needed to be sent back to the research and development department.

> *Hiroshi created competition among his inventors, but was also able to foster collaboration . . . crucially he had a real knack of knowing when a product would sell and when it needed to be sent back to the research and development department*

During the early 1970s Nintendo brought out playful devices such as the Ultra Hand, an extended false limb with a grasping hand on the end, The Ultra Machine, an indoor baseball pitcher and the Love Tester, an electronic device which purported to measure the love between a boy and a girl when they held hands. But in 1973 events abroad were to have a major impact on Nintendo and on the plans of companies across the world. The world's first oil shortage disrupted businesses everywhere. As the lights literally went out, shops closed and consumers cut back drastically on luxury goods. Nintendo saw its orders from customers slashed and Hiroshi had little choice but to reconsider his company's future. The possibility of complete collapse was very real. But in times of great upheaval businesses with weak leaders often fail while those with truly great leaders find a way through.

As it happened, the oil crisis coincided with major technological breakthroughs in microprocessors and semi-conductors, which led to the very first 'video games'. Companies such as Atari and Magnavox sprung up and started selling games consoles that could be hooked up to a television set. These were simple but really enjoyable games and were a major breakthrough in home entertainment. Nintendo agreed a deal with

Magnavox, signing up the rights to manufacture and sell *Pong* across Japan. It then formed an alliance with Mitsubishi to produce the consoles and in 1977 brought *Color TV Game 6* to Japan, selling over a million units. So after nearly 30 years at the helm of Nintendo, Hiroshi had finally found the type of products which were to make his company a household name across the world.

Trials and errors

The company began experimenting with mini-games devices and brought out a small novelty called Game & Watch, a precursor to the Game Boy. Hiroshi could see how great the potential of this new form of entertainment was, and was keen for Nintendo to become a major player in the video games industry. However at this stage, in the early 1980s, the company that just 10 years earlier had been making grabbing hands and toy guns was playing catch-up in an industry where businesses such as Atari and Commodore were already streets ahead. Hiroshi was inspired by new machines such as the Atari 2600; this featured a small box which plugged into customers' TV sets, and which had a slot to take cartridges with games on, expanding the number of games the machine could play significantly. He reckoned that the real way to make money was to base his business on the sale of games which could only be played on the machines he made. So he set his engineers a task: to create a console at less than a third of the price of other machines on the market and which could offer a better level of playability and graphics. 'Create something which other companies cannot make for at least one year. Make it so much better than that there will be no question which system the other customers will want,' he told them (*Game Over* by David Sheff, Random House 1993).

He set his engineers a task: to create a console at less than a third of the price of other machines on the market and which could offer a better level of playability and graphics

His engineers looked over the designs of their competitors and attempted to make improvements. They spent hours poring over calculations attempting to get the performance that Hiroshi was demanding. Eventually it was agreed that two chips would be needed, a central processing unit (CPU) and a picture processing unit (PPU). Also, it was agreed that the production of the chips needed to be outsourced. Hiroshi always drove hard bargains with his suppliers demanding more and more for less, so much so, in fact, that many chip makers simply wouldn't deal with Nintendo, as Nintendo was very demanding as a buyer in general and insisted on flexibility, which some companies couldn't cope with. On the question of chips Nintendo wanted a really low price and the only way it would make sense was if there was a high volume of orders. However, at this time the home video games market just wasn't that big and Nintendo's order of two million chips was far more than the whole of the existing Japanese market.

Nintendo approached Ricoh, who were going through a slow patch at the time and could therefore really do with the extra sales; but even it balked at the price offered. So Hiroshi proposed a deal which many thought was preposterous. He guaranteed Ricoh orders for three million chips over the next two years if it could produce at the price he requested. It was a massive gamble as the industry was still in its infancy and the overall size of the market was unknown. Certainly, this was far too many for the Japanese market alone and would require the company to embark on major international expansion. So the company set up an office in the USA and set about planning the launch of the new games machine there.

Hiroshi guaranteed orders for three million chips over the next two years; it was a massive gamble as the industry was still in its infancy

Nintendo had now designed a system which could carry most of the attributes which we recognise in the game systems available today. However, add-ons such as keyboards were not available for the first Nintendo Entertainment System (NES), or the Famicom (family computer) as it was known in Japan. This was because Hiroshi wanted to keep costs low and for the product to be as simple as possible. Still, as it started to present the new machine to its retail customers, they expressed serious reservations. They were concerned about its low price and their own small margins from each one – it seemed as though it would not be worth their while to stock the product. But Hiroshi insisted that the core machines must be sold cheaply and that the real money was to be made through the sale of games, and eventually managed to persuade them to stock it. 'The system is really just a tool to sell games, that is where we shall make our money,' he told them.

The NES was a massive hit in North America as well as Japan, and began to fly off the shelves, selling over half a million units in just six months. Game players enjoyed treats such as Donkey Kong, Metroid, The Legend of Zelda and Kid Icarus. The games were to cross new boundaries in computer gaming and saw off much of the competition in the sector. Now the imitator was to become the imitated.

However, there were bumps along the road to international success for Nintendo. Just six months after the first NES was released it emerged that a problem caused the consoles circuitry to freeze. Hiroshi ordered a complete recall which posed the risk of the company missing out on precious Christmas orders and allowing competitors valuable time to catch them up. But Hiroshi decided that if he allowed the problem to fester then it would damage Nintendo's reputation among consumers.

A new world

Nintendo's biggest hit, which would take it across the whole world, was a game called Super Mario Brothers. Mario was first seen as one of the characters in Donkey Kong. Interestingly, many of Nintendo's games salesmen were opposed to Donkey Kong which they thought sounded ridiculous; in fact it was supposed to be called Monkey Kong, which makes rather more sense, but a letter got changed in a classic mistranslation, and the rather more memorable Donkey Kong name was born. The game might never have seen the light of day had Hiroshi not had so much faith in the vision of one of his chief creatives, Shigeru Miyamoto. Shigeru was the brains behind many of Nintendo's greatest games drawing his inspiration from classical legends such as *King Kong*. Donkey Kong, which featured a cartoon character of a plumber trying to rescue a princess from a giant ape, proved to be a top seller. The character of the plumber, Mario, was further developed and given a brother, called Luigi, and the first of many Super Mario Bros games was born.

Super Mario was the driving force behind Nintendo. Between 1985 and 1991 eight versions of Super Mario were made and close to 70 million copies of the games were sold. Kids simply adored Super Mario and couldn't get enough of it. So much so that when Nintendo wanted to bring a new console to market it would package in the next version of Super Mario to ensure that parents of children bought the latest device. Mario was a key part in the development and growth of revolutionary consoles such as the Super NES, Nintendo 64 and Nintendo DS.

Kids only

Computer gaming often gets a bad press due to the adult content included in some games, which theoretically children can play. Nintendo has always steered clear of this by banning nudity or sexually explicit images from its games. Violent games, certainly those which contain gore, are also not allowed or are likely to be heavily toned down. The company's tight control over taste and decency has meant that there are some projects that it hasn't been able to do. This has left a gap in the market which others have been able to get into. As the gaming market has grown in maturity and its buyers have become older this might be seen by some as a mistake. Games such as Grand Theft Auto are now massive sellers and rivals such as Sony have been cashing in. Alternatively, Hiroshi's decision could have been a masterstroke. The popularity of Nintendo is dependent on the willingness of adults to purchase the consoles and games on behalf of their children. A moral outcry caused by a 'tasteless game' – particularly in a country such as the USA – could make parents far less willing to leave their children alone in the bedroom with a NES. In fact, Hiroshi might have made a smart call.

One of the other great ingredients of Nintendo's international success is how the company has consistently come out with innovative games which children love. Hiroshi himself must be given a considerable amount of credit for choosing the games that would really work well. He would personally decide whether or not a game would be allowed to be developed. He rated his own judgement far above that of the various marketing professionals and consumer testers. He believed that they could only tell him what was popular now and not what would be in the future. His creative research and development department were held in far greater esteem and brilliant men like Shigeru Miyamoto were able to thrive and prosper at Nintendo. Creating an environment which could nurture and harness such creativity is surely one of the great triumphs of Nintendo.

The company has consistently come out with innovative games which children love, while maintaining tight control over taste and decency

That's my boy

The other big success for Nintendo came in the late 1980s with the launch of the Game Boy. In a similar scheme to the other consoles, the device was not sold too expensively and the games were the real money makers. However, the target audience wasn't restricted to children, but also included adults. Passengers on longhaul flights, commuters going to the office and mothers waiting outside their child's school were all avid fans. Game Boy's greatest game was called Tetris, the infuriatingly addictive building block game, which has taken hours from the lives of so many people. The simple game was not impeded by the Game Boy's relatively low graphics, which were only in black and white when it was first launched. The Game Boy caused much consternation among Nintendo's competitors and once again spawned many imitators. However, efforts by Sega and others failed to match the Game Boy, which is still being sold today.

Where are they now?

Nintendo continued throughout the 1990s and into the early 21st century as an innovative and pioneering computer games business. In some ways the company has had little choice but to do so as the computer gaming industry is itself so dynamic. Also, rivals such as Sony have been keen to compete with Nintendo and oust them from the top spot. The NES and the Game Boy have both been developed considerably over the past 20 years. While there have been times when it has looked like Nintendo was about to lose its dominance among young gamers, the company has shown a habit for bouncing back. Sony's PlayStation 2 was more successful, for example, than Nintendo's

HOW **THEY** STARTED

Game Cube, leading some industry commentators to predict Nintendo's demise. But true to the heart of the company, Nintendo released the Wii console.

While Sony's PlayStation 3 and Microsoft's X-Box 360 both featured lots of extra technology to improve the graphics of their games, Nintendo chose a very different path. Their new console lets players control what happens on the screen by moving their control units around in the air, rather than just by hitting buttons on them. Motion technology such as this has been around for some years but Nintendo managed to significantly reduce its costs in order that it could be produced for the mass market, and also produce a range of games which take full advantage of the new control system. The result was that Nintendo's new console was substantially cheaper than Sony's or Microsoft's, and offered a very different game playing experience. It worked. Today, the company has sold over 25 million Wiis and has opened a new chapter in computer gaming.

Hiroshi stepped down as president of the company in 2002 and was succeeded by Satoru Iwata. He remained on the board until 2005 until ill health forced him to step down. Hiroshi is now the richest man in Japan and has retained a stake in the company until this day. He has used his enormous wealth to invest in things such as the US baseball team the Seattle Mariners, as well as humanitarian causes such as the Kyoto University Hospital. Shigeru Miyamoto is now managing director at Nintendo. He has won countless awards and is one of the most respected game designers in the industry. His oversight of the Wii project has only enhanced his reputation in the world of gaming to the extent that the industry is waiting desperately to see what he comes up with next.

Nokia

A GOOD CALL

Founder: Fredrik Idestam

Age of founder at start: 27

Background: Mining engineer and businessman

Year of foundation: 1865

Business type: Telecommunications manufacturer

Countries now trading in: 150

Turnover: £3.57bn ($6.25bn) (2007)

HOW **THEY STARTED**

The little tune which plays every time a Nokia phone rings must now be one of the best-known tunes in the world, being heard hundreds of millions of times every day. Nokia is the global market leader in mobile phone manufacturing with a staggering 40% market share despite plenty of substantial competitors.

Starting up

Nokia almost certainly has the least likely beginnings imaginable for a modern mobile phone company. Today's telecoms giant's ancestor business was conceived in relatively humble beginnings in 1865. This is when founder Fredrik Idestam successfully obtained a permit to build a wood pulp mill on the Tammerkoski river, by the small industrial town of Tampere in southern Finland.

The name 'Nokia' comes from the river which runs through Tampere. The river is called Nokianvirta, an old Finnish word which means 'marten', after the small, dark, furry animal which was once found in the region and which were commonly known as 'nokia'.

The mill did well, and was swiftly followed by a second mill on the Nokianvirta river, this time in a town called Nokia. Nokia provided better facilities for hydropower production, which was important for a wood pulp business. Its location proved useful in keeping labour costs low: the rivers' fertile banks enabled the company to actually grow food for its workforce. Soon, the business took on the name of the town, as happened often in that period (unlike today, companies were usually named after either their founders or their location).

Originally a mining engineer, Idestam brought a new, cheaper paper manufacturing process to Finland from Germany which proved highly successful. In doing so, he cemented his status as the so-called patriarch of the Finnish paper industry, which remains one of the world's major paper producers, with his invention being lauded at the Paris World Exposition in 1867 and winning the bronze medal.

Shortly afterwards, in 1871, Idestam legitimised his company's name, calling it Nokia Ab and moved its centre of operations to the town of Nokia.

Ringing out the changes

As it expanded, the company helped the town grow, with roads, bridges and later a telegraph office built in the factory premises (1877). A telephone line was also established between Tampere and Nokia. (It's not difficult to see where Nokia got its brand catchphrase, 'Connecting People', from.) By 1895, Nokia had its own railway station.

Idestam retired from the company in 1896, after more than 30 years leading the growing enterprise. Just two years later, in the first of many steps in becoming a multi-product conglomerate, Nokia Ab added electricity generation to the business mix to ensure its own supply in its remote location.

Meanwhile, in 1898, attracted by the rapid development and resources provided by the town of Nokia, the Finnish Rubber Works, founded by Arvid Wickström moved in; this would later form the basis of Nokia's own rubber business.

With business moving apace, in 1912 the Finnish Cable Works were founded by Eduard Polón in the town of Nokia. In what was to become a familiar pattern, this too laid the groundwork for Nokia's cable and electronics business. Houses were specifically built by the company for its ever increasing workforce and, ever progressive in their outlook, both the Nokia company and Finnish Rubber Works established vocational schools for both girls and boys.

Fredrik Idestam, who died on 8 April 1916, is gone, but not forgotten. Nokia Manor, his original home and now the occasional meeting place for Nokia's top management, is currently being excavated; archaeologists consider the site, which has seen activity across the stone, metal and middle ages, as being of important historical and archaeological value.

In 1922, investors in the Finnish Rubber Works, headed up by lead shareholder Oy Gottfried Strömberg Ab, bought the shares of the Finnish Cable Works, meaning that while they were still run as separate companies, all three companies in the town were

THE NOKIA COMPANY'S LOGO USED FROM 1966

now owned by the same investors. The businesses continued to grow, and managed to survive the Second World War intact.

In fact the Second World War ultimately proved helpful to the company. As part of Finland's war reparations to the Soviet Union, the Finnish Cable Company had to provide cable to the Soviet Union. At the time the Finnish Cable Company was headed up by a colourful character called Verner Weckman. Verner had been the Olympic Gold Medallist in 1906 in Athens, Finland's first ever Olympic Gold Medallist, in fact. After his sporting prowess, Verner went on to become a mining engineer, working extensively in Russia between 1906 and 1922, where he learned the language fluently and gained a great understanding about the culture of the Russian people. He went on to be technical director of the Finnish Cable Company for 10 years before being appointed chief executive. After the end of the war, Verner used his extensive knowledge of Russia to build a substantial export business to the country, its first foray into international expansion.

The Cable Works explored the boom in electronics with the establishment of its first electronics department in 1960, selling and operating computers. Just two years later, it had developed its first in-house electrical 'gadget': a pulse analyser for nuclear power plants. This period was key to Nokia's later development into a mobile power house; in 1963 it began to experiment with radio telephones for the army and emergency services and further develop its burgeoning communications expertise.

This period was key to Nokia's later development into a mobile power house; in 1963 it began to experiment with radio telephones for the army and emergency services

With this momentum building, the turning point for Nokia as a company finally arrived. Although they had been jointly owned since 1922, in 1967 came the formal merger of Nokia Ab (interestingly, the smallest of the three businesses at the time), Finnish Rubber Works and Finnish Cable Works, creating the Nokia Corporation. This corporation then operated in five key areas: rubber, cable, forestry, electronics and power generation. Industrialist Björn Westerlund was the firm's first president, taking over from Werner Weckman. Armed with a degree in electrical engineering from the Helsinki University of Technology, Westerlund is widely credited as laying the foundations for Nokia's dominance in the electronics and mobile sector.

THE DEVELOPMENT OF TECHNOLOGY: MOBIRA TALKMAN, NOKIA 8810, NOKIA 6110 AND MOBIRA CITYMAN

Ring it on!

Between 1968 and 1991, the newly formed Nokia Corporation was well positioned
for a pioneering role in the early evolution of mobile communications. As European
telecommunications markets were deregulated and mobile networks became global,
Nokia led the way with some iconic products. These included the Nordic Mobile
Telephone, the first international mobile phone network, built in 1981. The introduction
of the NMT (Nordic Mobile Telephone) standard meant that the mobile phone industry
began to expand rapidly. Initially spanning several Nordic countries, the NMT was the
world's first international cellular network and the first to allow international roaming
and caught on fast both inside and outside Europe.

Nokia soon introduced the first car phones to the network. The Mobira 450 car phone
came in 1982, followed by the portable Mobira Talkman in 1986. By this time the
company was also providing base stations and switches for NMT network operators. It
developed the Nokia DX200, its first digital telephone switch and the Mobira Cityman,
the first handheld NMT phone. In 1991, Nokia equipment was used to make the world's
first GSM phone call. GSM, The Global System for Mobile communications, was adopted
in 1987 as the European standard for digital mobile technology. This second generation
mobile technology could carry data as well as voice traffic. By the end of the 1990s, Nokia
had supplied GSM systems to more than 90 operators worldwide.

HOW **THEY** STARTED

As Nokia expanded into Asia, it ensured that the digit 4 never appeared in any Nokia handset model number, as in many areas, it is considered unlucky.

A good call

In terms of strategic development, 1992 was a pivotal year for Nokia. Not only did Nokia appoint Jorma Ollila as its new president and CEO, but it also decided to focus its future business development on the telecommunications side of the business. Accordingly, it gradually sold off its interests in rubber, cable and consumer electronics.

Prior to joining Nokia in 1985, Ollila, born in 1950, spent eight years in corporate banking at Citibank. He'd also accumulated master's degrees in economics, engineering and politics. He had been promoted to head of finance and chief of the mobile phone section in 1990.

The era of Ollila brought some calm to Nokia, following a period of internal fighting and financial problems. Tragically, the company's previous CEO, Kari Kairamo, had committed suicide in 1988, following a prolonged bout of manic depression. It's believed that heavy losses incurred by the television manufacturing division played a part in his decision to take his own life. With Ollila's long-term vision for the company came the end of some of the more historic elements of the business. The rubber, cable and consumer electronics sections were sold off gradually, allowing Nokia to invest heavily in mobile phones and the manufacture of telecommunication systems. The next few years proved a roll-call of innovative roll-outs from Nokia:

* 1992: Nokia launches its first GSM handset, the Nokia 1011
* 1994: Nokia launches the first phone to feature the Nokia Tuner and the world's first satellite call is made, using, (of course) a Nokia GSM handset
* 1998: Just six years following Ollila's appointment and subsequent strategic decision, Nokia was leading the world in mobile phones, selling more than any other company and winning praise in the global business press.

By 1998 Nokia was leading the world in mobile phones, selling more than any other company

In 2000 came the widely acknowledged telecoms industry crash. At the time, Ollila and his wife were refurbishing their 200-year-old home north of Helsinki. Instead of diving for cover, Ollila pushed ahead with his vision for Nokia. His determination has been noted in the press; *Time* magazine described Ollila in 2003 as a 'charming, bookish CEO', who has 'transformed the 136-year-old firm from a faceless conglomerate to a tech wunderkind'.

JORMA OLLILA (PRESIDENT AND CEO FROM 1992 to 2006) AND OLLI-PEKKA KALLASVUO (CEO FROM 2006)

A call to arms

In 2006, Olli-Pekka Kallasvuo, formerly Nokia's chief financial officer, took over as CEO from Jorma Ollila, who had served at Nokia for 13 years. Ollila became a part-time chairman of Nokia's board of directors, and also took on the roles of non-executive chairman of Royal Dutch Shell and the Ford Motor Company.

Born on 13 July 1953 in Lavia, Finland, Kallasvuo was very much a Nokia man. A 25-year Nokia veteran, he joined Nokia in 1980 as corporate counsel armed with a master's degree in law from Helsinki University and steadily but rapidly progressed up the company ranks.

It hadn't all been plain sailing during the reign of Ollila; he did preside over a difficult and extremely competitive time for the communications market and was occasionally the target of criticism. Analysts and investors have criticised Ollila for his reluctance to bring out new, all-singing, all-dancing models, at a time when competitors were introducing cameras, and music features.

However, it's tempting to suggest you'd be hard pressed to find a more suitable or experienced pair of hands for Ollila to hand over to. Kallasvuo, however, knew he had some big shoes to fill and wasn't complacent about it. 'Mr Ollila is a hard act to follow. But I am not looking back, I am looking forward to the tasks and challenges ahead,' Kallasvuo once told the *Financial Times*.

HOW **THEY** STARTED

NOKIA'S HEAD OFFICE IN ESPOO, FINLAND

True to his word, in 2006 Kallasvuo guided Nokia through a merger of its networks business and the carrier related operations of Siemens to create a new company, Nokia Siemens Networks. In his lighter moments, he admits to a love of golf, tennis and political history.

Where are they now?

With the ever-increasing media meshing of mobile communications with computing, digital imaging and the internet, Nokia positions itself firmly at the forefront of this converging industry and claims it will continue in its historic path of communication and cutting edge innovation. That's not to say the road may not be bumpy. In conversation on the topic of convergence in October 2006, Kallsavuo told the *Economist*: 'We have to be extremely careful that we don't go in the Swiss army knife kind of direction where we lose focus on what the consumer wants.'

And if numbers are anything to go by, the consumer is happy. In 2007, Nokia was heralded as the fifth most valued brand in the world. This coincided with the launch of Nokia Siemens Networks and the launch of Ovi, its new internet services brand. This continued development and innovation cements Nokia's well-deserved reputation as a true pioneer in telecommunications. From humble beginnings it is now the self-declared world leader in mobility, the world's largest camera manufacturer and a leader in digital music.

Nokia believes there will be around two billion mobile phone users at the end of 2008. It sees mobility as the fastest growing technology in the history of mankind. They also envisage around four billion people being connected by mobile devices by the end of 2009. Much of this enormous growth is coming from China, India and other fast-developing countries

THE MODERN ERA: NOKIA N96

where mobiles are becoming the core phone system, bypassing fixed line phones altogether for most of the population. Every third mobile sold in the world is a Nokia. In the second quarter of 2008, it enjoyed a 40% market share of the global device market. By far Finland's largest company, with its headquarters in Espoo, it accounts for a third of the market capitalisation of the Helsinki stock exchange. It had 112,000 employees at the end of 2007.

Nokia is now the self-declared world leader in mobility, the worlds largest camera manufacturer and a leader in digital music

It seems ironic that a company which began partly as a forestry business, inevitably a fairly slow-moving trade, and partly as a cable manufacturer is now poised for further substantial growth in one of the world's fastest moving sectors based on cable-free communication. Perhaps the ultimate proof that bold, agile businesses can turn threats into opportunities? One thing, though, seems sure: that the Nokia ringtone will be heard many more times over the coming years.

Sony

AN ELECTRIFYING BRAND

Founders: **Masaru Ibuka and Akio Morita**

Ages of founders at start: **38 and 25**

Background: **Engineering and family business, brewing sake**

Year of foundation: **1946**

Business type: **Consumer electronics**

Countries now trading in: **More than 150**

Turnover: **£47bn ($88bn)**

HOW **THEY** STARTED

Not many people will be familiar with the Japanese firm Tokyo Tsushin Kogyo but they will almost certainly have heard of Sony, the company it became. Founded more than half a century ago by friends Masaru Ibuka and Akio Morita, the company's first innovation was an electrical rice cooker. These days, Sony is famed for products that are far more sexy and glamorous. Many have revolutionised the way technology is being used by consumers and today, Sony's inventions entertain millions of people around the world. With iconic products including WALKMAN, PlayStation, VAIO laptops and the MiniDisc, it is one of the best-known brands in consumer electronics. It has also made a name for itself in the music, motion picture and television businesses.

A meeting of minds

As a child, Masaru was highly inquisitive, fond of experimenting with different types of technology and an avid radio ham. His passion for innovation did not go unnoticed at university, where he earned the nickname 'genius inventor'. After graduating from the School of Science and Engineering at Tokyo's Waseda University in 1933, one of the country's top academic institutions, he worked at various companies over the next 12 years, specialising in sound recording and telecommunications.

By 1945 Japan was emerging from the shadow of the Second World War and economic times were tough. These were hardly the best conditions in which to contemplate starting a business, but for Masaru the lure of being able to experiment with technology was temptation enough. With some of his own savings, he opened a radio repair shop, Tokyo Tsushin Kogyo (which translates as Tokyo Telecommunications Engineering Company), in a bombed-out department store in Tokyo. A year later, he was joined by Akio, who had spotted an article in the newspaper about the growth in popularity of radios, and which mentioned Masaru. Both men had previously met during the war and struck up a friendship, when Akio had served as an officer in the Japanese Imperial Navy and Masaru was working as a civilian radio engineer.

Akio needed little persuasion to join the business and he and Masaru went into partnership, stumping up capital of around $500 (which is £2,985 or $5,257 today) towards the business and recruiting employees. Akio was born into a prominent sake-brewing family in Nagoya, Japan's fourth largest city, and was expected to take over the 400-year-old family business. In true entrepreneurial spirit, however, he turned his back on a secure lifestyle in favour of a more risky venture.

Each complemented the other as Masaru specialised in telecommunications and educational electronics, often taking gadgets apart on the office floor to learn how they worked, while Akio focused on the marketing and branding side of the business. They sought to create products where the best technology was matched with the highest quality. The company's first invention, an electric rice cooker, launched in the late 1940s, but it failed commercially as the rice was either under or overcooked. This may have been a blessing in disguise, as it was to be in communications rather than cookery where Masaru and Akio really made their mark. In its first year the business registered a profit of $300 on sales of less than $7,000.

They sought to create products where the best technology was matched with the highest quality, but it was to be in communications rather than cookery where they made their mark

Perseverance pays off

As the Japanese economy began to revive and demand for consumer goods increased, Masaru and Akio decided to abandon the home appliance market in favour of what they liked and knew best – electronic goods. Masaru had prepared a prospectus for the company where he had communicated his vision. 'We must avoid problems which befall large corporations, while we create and introduce technologies which large corporations cannot match', it said.

In 1950, following an injection of capital from Akio's father, the pair came up with their initial electronic hardware device – the first tape player and recorder in Japan, which they called the G-Type. What it had in terms of technology it lacked in design – it was big and bulky and the resulting clumsy look meant that it, too, flopped commercially. Unlike the rice cooker, Masaru and Akio were determined to make this device sell.

Sales remained stagnant until by chance, Masaru uncovered a US military booklet entitled *Nine hundred and ninety-nine uses of the tape recorder*. They translated this into Japanese, and distributed it as widely as they could. The booklet did a most effective job as a marketing tool for the business and sales of the tape recorder increased dramatically, so much so that the company was forced to move to bigger offices.

At the heart of the business, however, lay product innovation and it wasn't long before Masaru started experimenting with other formats, turning his attention to transistors. These had originally been developed by US-based research organisation Bell Laboratories, while a company called Western Electric had purchased the technology. Other US firms had already built transistor radios but these were mainly for use in military applications. In the early 1950s Masaru travelled to the USA and spotted an opportunity for transistors in the commercial market. He convinced Bell to license the technology to his company for $25,000, with the aim of creating a small, tubeless radio. A few months later, in 1954, Masaru and Akio began mass rollout of transistor radios.

Akio too had returned from his first trip to the USA and came back with a lot more than he bargained for – a company name change. He realised that the business would need a name that could be both recognised and pronounced outside Japan. A three-letter abbreviation of the company name to TTK had already been ruled out as it was already in use by another Japanese company. Inspiration came from the business itself – Sony was derived from the Latin term 'sonus', the root of the words sonic and sound, and the expression `Sonny-boys', Japanese slang for whiz-kids. It encapsulated both the company's products and the creativity behind them.

The road to growth

In 1955, the company produced its first coat-pocket-sized transistor radio, registering it under the TR-55 model, with the name Sony being used as a trademark on the product for the first time. The Japanese were still struggling with the aftermath of the war and couldn't afford expensive electronics, so the pair decided to target the USA and its stronger economy. Global expansion, to a certain extent, was borne out of necessity. 'I knew we needed a weapon to break through to the US market and it had to be something different, something that nobody else was making,' Akio said in a later interview with *Time* magazine. First attempts to get into the US market backfired, however. Wholesalers had little enthusiasm for the product, arguing that while small products were popular in Japan, consumers in the USA liked them on the larger side.

Sony was derived from the Latin term 'sonus', the root of the words sonic and sound, and the expression 'Sonny-boys', Japanese slang for whiz-kids

Refusing to take no for answer, Masaru and Akio persevered, coming up with different types of transistor models. Eventually, Sony received an order for 100,000 units from established US watchmaker Bulova, under the condition that the radios carried the latter's name, rather than Sony's. Akio refused – after all, the company's ethos was to innovate and Akio wanted to develop their own brand, not make products for another company. Instead, he accepted more modest orders, which enabled the company to grow at a more moderate, but sensible rate. It was a decision Akio would later recall as the best one he had ever made. In 1956, they made and sold around 40,000 portable transistor radios, and demand slowly picked up. They began to export transistor radios to the Netherlands and Germany, too, as well as the USA.

In his autobiography, Akio admitted that he couldn't quite get the radios small enough to fit inside a shirt pocket, but ever the creative thinker, he simply ordered shirts with bigger pockets for the company's salesmen, to give the impression of a smaller radio.

In 1957, the company produced the smallest transistor radio in commercial production at the time. Measuring 112 x 71 x 32mm, it became an instant worldwide success, cracking the US teen market. In part, uptake was due to the emergence of rock 'n' roll music, as teens from all over the USA rushed to buy portable radios. The figures speak for themselves – in 1955 an estimated 100,000 portable radios had been sold. By 1958, this number had swelled to five million. This year the company officially changed its name to Sony Corporation.

On a roll

Just one year later, Sony announced that it had developed a transistorised television, which was launched 12 months later. Following a dispute with Delmonico International, the company appointed to handle Sony's overseas sales, Masaru and Akio decided to open the company's first overseas offices, establishing one in New York and another in Switzerland. In 1961, the company floated on the US stock market, the first Japanese company to do so. Akio took global expansion one step further in 1963, when he moved to the USA for just over a year, reasoning that to sell effectively to Americans, he would have to know more about them and how they lived. It proved to be a shrewd move as Akio built lasting relationships with executives from some of the largest US corporations. These played a key part in forming Sony's later joint ventures. It was also the first step towards building an international network as Sony subsequently expanded its production facilities worldwide through more than 100 subsidiaries and affiliated companies.

The company continued to break ground on the back of transistor technology. Sony became known as a company at the forefront of modern technology and innovation after innovation swiftly followed, including an AM/FM radio and a videotape recorder, both introduced in the early 1960s. Towards the end of the decade, Sony engineers had developed colour television technology, a first for its time, which they named Trinitron. They also continued to expand around the world, and in 1968 Sony established an office in England and entered into a joint venture with phonograph firm CBS, which was later to become the largest record manufacturer in Japan. In 1974, Sony became the first major Japanese company to open a factory in the UK.

This international expansion was matched by further product inventions. One of Sony's next product launches was the video cassette recorder (VCR) in Betamax format, which launched in 1975. VCRs soon become big business but it wasn't all good news as competitors such as Toshiba had launched their own product using the technology Sony had once pioneered, causing it to lose market share.

Tough times

Sony's investment in research and development however, was strong. In July 1979, Sony unveiled its personal stereo – WALKMAN, but to start with, major electrical retailers showed little interest. Eight out of 10 Sony dealers were sceptical about its consumer appeal, believing that a cassette player without a recording mechanism would have a limited shelf life. Sales to start with were slow, with only 3,000 units sold in the launch month, so Sony decided that people would need to listen to the product to appreciate the sound.

They targeted young people at high school and college festivals, and the product gained momentum through word of mouth. Critics were proved wrong yet again as WALKMAN became a huge success, both at home and abroad. In an article in *New Scientist* magazine, Akio said: 'Technology is not everything. What is also needed is creative marketing. WALKMAN was not creative technology, but it created an enormous market.' Ten years after launch of the first model, more than 50 million units had been manufactured. By 1982, Sony had applied its creative marketing yet again, with the introduction of the world's first compact disc player.

'Technology is not everything. What is also needed is creative marketing. Walkman was not creative technology, but it created an enormous market.'

Undoubtedly, the company's success thus far had largely been attributed to its ability to introduce products ahead of the competition. Akio too, had an unusual knack that enabled him to anticipate and create markets for new products, but the company came under increasing threat from the competition. This wasn't, however, the only factor eroding Sony's dominant position in the consumer electronics market. It had failed to make its products the industry standard by encouraging other companies to participate in their creation and the consequences of this were soon felt.

Rival firm Matsushita Electric, which owned half of JVC, had developed a separate format for VCRs, called VHS, which was not compatible with Betamax. The company launched an aggressive marketing campaign to persuade consumers and manufacturers to embrace the format, suggesting that Betamax would soon be obsolete. A marketing war between the two companies ensued which neither benefitted from as both were forced to lower prices. Although Betamax's technology was generally considered to be superior, it was the VHS format that ultimately proved the more popular, as there were many more films available for purchase or rental on VHS than there were on Betamax. It wasn't until the late 1980s that Sony adopted the format, but not without first having lost substantial market share.

New directions

By the late 1970s, Masaru, who was nearing the age of 70, had passed many of his duties over to younger managers, although he continued to work as an advisor to the company until he died of heart failure in 1997. One of Sony's rising stars was Norio Ohga, who was to become president of the company in 1982. Akio too, reduced his responsibilities and under the leadership of Norio, Sony entered a new phase, eager to avoid the mistakes made with Betamax.

In 1985, it introduced a first video camera to the market, which is capable of recording video on standard 8mm videotape developed together with more than 100 competitors. While it was not compatible with either VHS or Betamax format, Sony had ensured the technology would work with the next generation of video cameras, thereby protecting itself for the future rather than the short term. It was a shrewd move – within three years of launch, the camera had captured 50% of the market in Europe, 30% in North America and 20% in Japan.

Norio had also learnt from past experience that a superior product on its own was not enough and started to identify potential acquisitions. In 1984, Sony purchased Apple Computers' hard disk technology operations, enabling it to capture 20% of the market for office computers in Japan. Three years later, Sony purchased CBS Records for $2bn ($3.7bn or £2bn today), in an attempt to gain a dominant position in the software part of the electronic and entertainment industries. It wanted to ensure that the products Sony manufactured for music would remain compatible in the long term with the medium used to record music.

It wasn't until 1989, however, that Sony completed a takeover that was to make all the headlines mainly because of the price paid – the acquisition of Columbia Entertainment from Coca-Cola Enterprises for $3.4bn ($6bn or £3bn today). The deal offered Sony access to an extensive film library and a strong US distribution system, but it also came saddled with debt to the tune of around $1bn. Paying interest on this debt was one of a number of factors which made the early 1990s into quite a struggle for Sony.

Global challenges

Things were particularly tough among Sony's worldwide enterprises. In the early 1990s, with a recession hitting many of the world's largest economies, Sony's operating income came under threat, particularly with the ongoing appreciation of the Japanese yen against most major currencies. In 1993, its net income plunged 70% to $313m (£188m) on sales of $516bn (£34.4bn).

At this point, Norio assumed chairmanship of Sony and Akio was made honorary chairman, having suffered a stroke in 1993. Nobuyuki Idei took over as president, having previously helped to establish the company's French division nearly 30 years earlier. Despite the injection of a new management team, Sony's electronic business continued to decline but a foray into the gaming industry did much for its reputation and its bottom line.

Playing forward

In 1991, Sony, an effective newcomer to the video gaming industry, had begun talks with Japanese gaming manufacturer Nintendo, with plans to create a PlayStation that would connect to Nintendo's entertainment system. The deal faltered twice, however, due to a conflict of vision and Sony was left to develop the video game system on its own. It was a strategy, though, that would pay off. Sony introduced the PlayStation in 1994 and backed by a strong advertising campaign, it was officially launched in the USA a year later. Conscious of avoiding the mistakes of the Betamax system, Sony courted independent computer games publishers for years before launching the PlayStation, and ensured that a good range of strong games would be available for the launch. It also set up and acquired its own computer games development studios in order to have greater control over the software side of the business — and to make the high profits that can come from successful games. The PlayStation was an instant success, selling out many times over. Within a few years it, and its sequel the PlayStation 2, dominated the market; Sony had beaten the giants of video games console manufacturing – Nintendo and Sega – at their own game.

> *The PlayStation was an instant success, selling out many times over. Within a few years it, and its sequel the PlayStation 2, dominated the market.*

The personal computer business was Sony's next target and in 1997, very late in the development of the PC market, it began selling its VAIO line of PCs. Although no one could fault the quality of the unusually stylish computers, high prices meant sales were slow. In 1999, Akio died after suffering from pneumonia and it heralded a change in direction for the business, with Nobuyuki Idei aiming to position Sony for 'the network era of the 21st century'. By October 2001, it had formed a joint venture with Ericsson to manufacture mobile phones, competing with mobile heavyweights Nokia and Motorola, and setting up global headquarters in London.

But Sony did not grasp every major new development in consumer electronics. It had missed out on the early years of the PC market, was slow to spot the potential of MP3 players and failed to exploit the opportunities offered by the internet, leaving competitors such as Apple to launch enormously successful products such as the iPod. Sony also once lost market share in the television sector as it failed to capitalise on new flat-screen technology, resulting in sluggish sales.

Where are they now?

In 2005, Idei stepped down as chairman and group chief executive officer, and Howard Stringer, then chairman and CEO of Sony Corporation of America assumed the mantle. His appointment marked the first time a foreigner had run a major Japanese electronics firm. He set about restructuring the business to revive its flagging fortunes, by concentrating on improving three core areas: electronics, games and entertainment.

In recent years, along with nearly every other player in the electronics industry, Sony has been striving to bridge the gap between computers and televisions. But 2008 might just be the year it brings the two together. It has been heavily promoting the Blu-ray disc format, which has the backing of major motion picture studios. It was a hard-won battle, as Sony went head to head with Toshiba, which announced earlier this year that it would be abandoning its HD offering. Sony is also looking at new opportunities, such as increasing the video content on its devices and exploring the business-to-business market. It unveiled its first VAIO range for the corporate market earlier this year.

And Sony's newest games console, PlayStation 3, has begun selling more slowly than expected, due to its high price, the result of a very advanced technical specification, and the success of the very different competition from Nintendo's Wii console. Knowing Sony, though, this competitive battle is far from over.

So Sony, as with all companies, needs to adapt to a world where it won't necessarily come up with every great new idea, and instead needs to find a way of thriving in an ever more competitive world. This mirrors Akio's original core philosophy, perhaps described best in his autobiography, *Made in Japan* (HarperCollins Publishers 1994): 'If you go through life convinced that your way is always best, all the new ideas in the world will pass you by.'

'**Sony**', '**WALKMAN**' and '**VAIO**' are registered trademarks of Sony Corporation.

'PlayStation', 'PlayStation 2' and 'PlayStation 3' are registered trademarks of Sony Computer Entertainment Inc.

All other trademarks are property of their respective owners.

Bebo

A SOCIAL PHENOMENON

Founders: **Michael and Xochi Birch**

Age of founders at start: **35 and 33**

Background: **Insurance and online ventures**

Year of foundation: **2005**

Business type: **Social networking site**

Country of foundation: **UK**

Countries now trading in: **7; soon to launch in 5 more**

Turnover and profit: **Not available**

HOW **THEY** STARTED

Websites such as Facebook, MySpace and YouTube have exploded in popularity over the last few years, growing from almost nothing to having hundreds of millions of regular users today, especially among the under-30 age group. You would be forgiven for thinking that this internet phenomenon was a purely American invention. But you'd be mistaken.

Bebo, the UK-founded social networking website, has a total membership of more than 45 million worldwide. So just how did Michael Birch, the site's founder, begin the Bebo phenomenon in 2005?

Network knowledge

Michael believes the idea behind Bebo was straightforward: to 'give people want they want and not something they don't want'. That sounds simple enough, but Bebo's success was also the result of a long process of trial and error for Michael. Since quitting his IT job at an insurance company, Bebo was Michael's sixth venture. For him, it was a three-year learning curve before he found success. Three ventures had failed and two were moderate successes before Bebo came on the scene. Michael is philosophical about his earlier ventures' mixed fortunes: 'It's a learning experience but just because something fails, it isn't necessarily a complete waste; you learn what you can from it, realise one element that works well, and leverage that into a new business.'

Michael's ventures were all online. He knew from an early age that he wanted to start and run his own business, and the arrival of the internet provided the impetus, and more importantly, the platform he needed. He explains, 'I quickly realised this was the perfect medium to be entrepreneurial – and I already had half the equation because I understood the IT side of it.' Armed with a background in computers, the internet was his proverbial oyster.

Just because something fails, it isn't necessarily a complete waste; you learn what you can from it

Stumbling upon success

One of Michael's earlier websites, BirthdayAlarm.com, which alerts the user of key dates like birthdays or anniversaries by email, met with some success. Once this was up and running, Michael started noticing a new breed of site emerging.

He was fascinated with the first social networks such as Sixdegrees.com (1997–2001) and had ideas on how that content could be improved. So, in 2003, with help from his team at BirthdayAlarm.com, he designed a photo-orientated social network called Ringo.com.

FOUNDERS MICHAEL AND XOCHI BIRCH

Michael's ventures were all online . . . the arrival of the internet provided the impetus, and more importantly, the platform he needed

HOW **THEY** STARTED

This proved an instant success to the point that Michael was unprepared for its growth. Aware of this, and of the high cost of supporting a fast-growing site like this, he decided to sell – just three months after starting it. 'We just couldn't afford to throw resources at it, we'd had three offers in a week and it was the hot property of the time,' he recalls about himself and his wife and business partner Xochi. 'It was then the second biggest social network next to Friendster. We decided to sell and focus on other things we were running at the time.' A shrewd move, considering many website startups fail as they can't cope with the rapid expansion that is expected of them. Interestingly, in June 2008, Ringo.com shut its doors to the internet traffic.

For those of you that don't know what social networking sites are, they involve a website where anyone can register and set up their own profile page. These profile pages tell anyone who cares to notice what the registered member likes and dislikes; members can talk to eac h other, and use their likes and dislikes to find other people with similar interests to talk to online. Some sites allow registered members to load photos and video clips of themselves, or things they like, onto their own pages. Social networking online forms a large part of what is now being referred to as 'web 2.0', a term covering a new generation of websites which offer far greater interactivity than witnessed in the first generation of the internet.

The birth of Bebo

Michael had to let Ringo.com go, but he wasn't finished with social networking, which was continuing to build momentum as household internet connections approached, for the first time, a critical mass. 'They were still early days for social networking, but I started to see how people interacting with each other could integrate with other types of media, such as music and video and how whatever suddenly becomes hot – such as blogging – fits easily into it. I found it completely fascinating that people were connecting in such a positive way and thought it had immense power and endless opportunity.'

Having played around with a number of emerging social networks, Michael sat down with a blank piece of paper to produce what, in his eyes, would be the ultimate network. It emerged initially as a photo-sharing network, but quickly evolved into a broader social networking site by the time his non-compete clause from the sale of Ringo.com had expired.

Standing out from the crowd

Michael was aware he had to enter the market with a unique proposition. For him, it was to address the youth market with a product that matched their demands for this sort of website, based on a strong understanding of exactly what they did, and equally importantly did *not*, want from a social networking website.

'I started to see how people interacting with each other could integrate with other types of media'.

Michael decided that this meant not excluding anyone by being too niche, and not being too complicated or as feature-heavy as some competitors. 'It's designed to be simple to use. You can register, get a homepage and be up-and-running in minutes.

THE HOMEPAGE THAT GREETS BEBO USERS

There is a depth of features, but you don't need to use them. Other sites put people off by being too tricky.'

The second fundamental issue for Michael was to create an environment to harbour and encourage a network. The idea was to create a 'healthy community' without trying to dictate how that community behaves. The internet-savvy youth market can be a harsh critic and Michael placed far more emphasis on providing the right environment than on an all-singing, all-dancing design. He aimed to set it apart with its modest aesthetics and simple functionality, thus seamlessly encouraging users onto the site. He comments that 'it was absolutely crucial that we weren't too corporate,' as this can alienate the younger demographic that thrives off freedom of expression and the identity that comes from creating their profile.

Guerrilla marketing

Not being 'too corporate' meant mass advertising the site was a no-go. Successful social networking sites tend to evolve on their own merits – not because a billboard and a million flashing banner ads say it's a great place to visit. Michael comments that 'it's almost impossible to contrive a natural-feeling social network by driving people there'.

So, when Bebo went live in July 2005, there was almost no launch advertising or marketing activity. There was a link up on BirthdayAlarm.com for two days, but then the site relied on targeted PR activity and the power of word of mouth, or rather, the power of a click of the mouse; as Michael describes, 'we literally just seeded it with the first few people and then it just grew on its own'. And boy did it grow.

Rocketing

They paid £4,500 ($8,000) for the domain name Bebo, because it was snappy, available and meaningless. (Now it is often said to stand for 'Blog early, blog often') Leaning heavily on the established site BirthdayAlarm.com, Bebo's startup costs were minimal, and remarkably, within two months, it was cashflow positive because of revenue generated from advertising.

Michael and Xochi used agencies to sell advertising for them, paying them a percentage of every sale, which enabled them to keep Bebo's running costs low and also freed them up to concentrate on building the site. This model also allowed them to sell advertising in different countries (by finding agencies in each country to sell advertising for them) even though they were only based in one – which was important since Bebo soon had substantial numbers of users all over the world.

In fact, international expansion was a very clear strategy for Bebo from the start. Interestingly, they initially focused on a number of countries other than the USA, as

Michael and Xochi believed there to be more untapped demand in places like Australia and their native Great Britain. They wanted to have strong roots before going all out to build an American presence.

Only 10 months after its inception, in May 2006, Bebo was voted Best Social Networking Website by more than 300,000 voters in the annual US People's Voice awards. At the end of 2006, the Year-End Google Zeitgeist announced that 'Bebo' was the number one search term of the year. Bebo had firmly established itself as one of the world's leading social networking sites. It had grown to 28 full-time staff, was receiving over five billion page impressions a month, and was ready to take it to the next level.

Even though it was cashflow positive, Michael and Xochi could see that maintaining the very rapid pace of growth would need more capital than they had. It was time for a cash injection, and in May 2006, venture capitalist Benchmark invested £7,824m ($15m) for an undisclosed slice of equity. This gave Bebo a great financial base to grow aggressively when they felt the timing was right, without having to go through drawn-out money raising processes first.

The rise of Bebo

In early 2007, Bebo took major steps towards solidifying its position at the top of the social networking charts, in particular strengthening its senior management. In January, Michael and Xochi appointed Joanna Shields (formerly managing director of strategic partnerships for Google Europe, Russia, Middle East & Africa) as president. Joanna's job was very specific: to expand Bebo's business. This appointment marked a significant advance in Bebo's commercial focus and plans for growth into other markets.

At the forefront of expansion plans was the web's first ever interactive online series, KateModern, announced in April 2007. Following the success of an online drama called lonelygirl15 on YouTube (which achieved 50 million hits across the summer of 2006), Joanna was quick to recognise the new 'social media' that was emerging, as young people spent less time watching TV and more time on the net sharing ideas, photos and music. Her intention was to bring this new online phenomenon to Bebo through online media. At a time when people doubted the staying power of social networking, Bebo was careful to ensure it cultivated new forms of interaction.

Commissioned by Bebo and co-developed with production company EQAL, it was launched in July 2007, and using Bebo's forums and devices, fans interact with the show's characters and even affect the outcome of storylines. Joanna was right on the money: Bebo's new series received 100,000 hits in its opening weekend, with no pre-marketing.

The series was funded almost solely by product placement. The writers would write specific brands and products into the storyline, and companies such as Procter &

CEO JOANNA SHIELDS JOINED BEBO IN EARLY 2007, AND HAS TAKEN THE SITE TO NEW HEIGHTS

Gamble (Gillette, Tampax and Pantene), MSN, Orange Mobile, Paramount and Disney/ Buena Vista paid £250,000 ($480,000) each for six months of plot integrations into KateModern. As predicted, KateModern was an immediate success; gaining 1.5 million viewers in the first week, and 35 million views through the first series. The second series ended in June 2008, with more than 67 million views, and Bebo is planning more online series for the future.

A definite shift from Michael's initial vision of a simple, no-frills site, Bebo has had to move with the times, to ensure it remains an internet pioneer

Standing out from the crowd

In July 2006, they launched a new service, Bebo Music, where musicians can upload their own music, followed by Bebo Books in February 2007, where authors upload chapters of their book, get critiques and comments. Covering yet more ground in the new 'social media' era, Bebo's management team realised that users were consuming over a billion videos a month from YouTube and other sites, but found it hard to find and share content from their favourite media brands, so in November 2007 Bebo's Open Media platform was launched.

Media companies were now able to embed their own video content into Bebo's social networking environment. The likes of MTV, Warner Brothers, Sky, ITN and some 400 other publishers have complete control over what clips – or whole programmes – they collate on Bebo's network. And if those clips carry advertising – pre-roll, mid-roll or banner ads within the media player – they retain 100% of those ad revenues. Bebo's strategy was totally different to that being deployed by any other social network or video distribution service.

According to Joanna, 'the spectrum of social networking is evolving beyond utilities and applications. Bebo is now a 'Social Media Network' where culture and content come together and people use media and entertainment as a means of self-expression.'

This unprecedented fusion of media ensured Bebo offered its users a unique service, and served well to stay off the rise of rival sites. Joanna has likened rival social networking website Facebook to a BlackBerry, while she says Bebo is a state-of-the-art Apple iPod Touch in terms of its media capabilities.

Open Media was the culmination of a gradual expansion in what the site offered its users. A definite shift from Michael's initial vision of a simple, no-frills site, Bebo has had to move with the times, to ensure it remains an internet pioneer. It still remains, however, centered on community: Open Media and other devices would not be anything like as successful without the natural, unforced communication among its users.

Breaking down the language barrier

As it stands, Bebo's presence is largest in the six English-speaking regions: the USA, Canada, the UK, Ireland, Australia, and New Zealand. In late 2007, Bebo launched a Polish version of the site, which is fully translated and tailored to the Polish community. In order to achieve this, Bebo partnered with Poland's leading media company, Agora, who took on the work of developing and promoting Bebo in Poland. By partnering with this media giant, Bebo was able to gain essential market knowledge, and could draw on Agora's already extensive reach and influence in Poland. Agora also took on the majority of ad sales, meaning that again, Bebo benefitted from their established contacts. This shrewd move made Bebo's expansion into different languages relatively seamless. Bebo has plans to continue its expansion into Europe during the final quarter of 2008, beginning with five countries: France, Germany, Spain, Italy and the Netherlands.

Where are they now?

Bebo is the number one social networking site in the British Isles (with more than 11.9 million UK users and 1.3 million users in Ireland). It's number one in New Zealand, number two in Australia, and number three in the USA and Canada.

In March 2008, Bebo was bought by AOL for £417m ($850m) and became part of AOL's newly created People Networks. Founders Michael and Xochi stepped away from the company, while Joanna was made CEO of Bebo, president of People Networks and executive vice president of AOL.

HOW **THEY** STARTED

The People Networks unit of AOL combines a collection of community platforms including Bebo, the AIM and ICQ personal communications network, widget technology company Goowy Media and social search and answer service Yedda. Together, the network reaches over 80 million unduplicated users worldwide.

'The third age (of the internet) is the most exciting and involves the biggest shift of power and potential of the internal so far'

As for Bebo's future plans, Joanna comments: 'We are well and truly in the third age of the internet. I think we can say the first age was about getting people connected to the web, enabling communications, laying infrastructure to support the future. When the original web portals AOL, Yahoo and MSN reigned supreme.

The second stage was about gathering information and giving people access to it. This stage of course was dominated by Google and they continue to hold strong in this sector of organising the world's information and making it accessible and useful.

But this third age is the most exciting and involves the biggest shift of power and potential of the internet so far because it is about creating a community and enhancing our lives online. At the heart of this third age are social networks, such as Bebo, which are becoming the central point from which people experience the web.'

Bebo's founder, Michael Birch plans to take a break from the social networking scene, concentrating instead on investing in startup companies – an entrepreneur at heart – as well as investing time in his family.

Bebo received the Innovation Award for Outstanding Development in Broadcasting at the 2008 Broadcast Press Guild Awards and secured two BAFTA nominations for its original programme KateModern.

eBay

BUYING POWER

Founder: Pierre Omidyar

Age of founder at start: 28

Background: Software engineer

Year of foundation: 1995

Business type: Online auction site

Countries now trading in: Branded sites in 39 markets

Turnover: $2.2bn (£1bn)

HOW **THEY** STARTED

Fifteen dollars might seem an insignificant amount, but it was the sum of money that sparked the business known today as eBay. Founder Pierre Omidyar, a software engineer, was experimenting with online auctions as a hobby and advertised a broken laser pointer for sale. He was amazed that someone would consider paying just under $15 ($14.83 to be precise) for an item that didn't work, and it convinced him that there was potential in a business catering to people's passion for collecting. The item was duly sold and dispatched and has gone down in history as eBay's first transaction. Today, the site, which is the world's largest online market place, is one of the most successful companies of the dotcom era and is still making headlines around the world.

Technology guru

Born in Paris, Pierre's family moved to Washington DC in 1973 when he was just six, and he became fascinated with computers and technology from an early age. While other kids were out playing sports, he was more likely to be found indoors, tinkering with hardware and learning how to programme computers. He taught himself to program in BASIC and used his technology skills to get his first job, computerising his school library's card catalogue system for $6 an hour. In *The Perfect Store: Inside eBay* (Adam Cohen, Piatkus Books 2003), a book charting eBay's history, Pierre recalls that he 'was your typical nerd or geek in high school.'

Unsurprisingly, Pierre decided to specialise in computer science at Tufts University near Boston in the 1980s, where he nurtured a passion for Apple Mac software. It was an early sign of his entrepreneurial flair and his desire to do something different. At the time, Apple was seen as a trendy and non-traditional technology company, a minnow challenging established giants such as IBM. Pierre's personal style of long hair tied back in a ponytail, beard and aviator-style glasses was well suited to his love of all things Apple.

In the late 1980s and early 1990s, he worked as a Macintosh programmer, securing a number of jobs at software companies in Silicon Valley before deciding to strike out on his own. Together with friends, he founded Ink Development Corporation, which aimed to produce software for pen-based computers, a forerunner to the Palm Pilot. This part of the business, however, did not take off as rapidly as he hoped and a year later, Pierre decided to focus on another offshoot from the business – online commerce. The company was subsequently renamed eShop, and operated as an electronic retailing company. While the concept of the internet was gathering momentum around the world, the pace of technology was still going too slowly for Pierre's liking and he quit eShop in 1994 in search of a business that would get him that one step closer to the internet. Pierre retained a stake in eShop though and in hindsight, this proved to be a very wise move. Barely two years later, it caught the attention of software giant Microsoft, and was subsequently acquired, making Pierre a millionaire before he turned 30.

FRENCH–BORN IRANIAN–AMERICAN PIERRE OMIDYAR, FOUNDER OF EBAY

While the concept of the internet was gathering
momentum, the pace of technology was still going too slowly
for Pierre's liking and he quit eShop in search of a business
that would get him that one step closer to the internet

All things internet

By then, Pierre had clearly caught the internet bug and luckily he was in the right place at the right time as a host of other online businesses were starting to emerge. Pierre developed his interest in all things internet by joining mobile communications startup General Magic. It was during his time here that the idea for AuctionWeb, which was to eventually become eBay, took shape. Like many great business ideas, Pierre's creation stemmed from a bad personal experience. A few years before, he had placed an order online for shares in a company that looked promising, but he discovered that the stock had soared by 50% before his order had been realised.

He thought it unfair that some buyers were favoured with one price, while others had to settle for another. He believed an online auction was a better way of arriving at a fairer price for all concerned and with the development of the internet, such a concept could become a reality. 'I've got a passion for solving a problem that I think I can solve in a new way', he once said in an interview. He wanted to test the potential of the web's ability to connect people around the world and offer a platform where buyers and sellers could share information about prices and products.

'I've got a passion for solving a problem that I think I can solve in a new way'

'Instead of posting a classified ad saying I have this object for sale, "give me $100", you post it and say "here's a minimum price"', he recalled in *The Perfect Store*. 'If there's more than one person interested, let them fight it out.'

The bigger picture

It was going to take time and patience to develop, but Pierre relished such a challenge and worked round the clock, holding down his day job during the week and working on AuctionWeb during his spare time in the evenings and at weekends – in fact, he wrote the initial code for Auction Web in one weekend. It was a labour of love and an all-consuming hobby; with his concept for an online auction, Pierre wanted, above all, to promote the idea of a community on the web, one which was built on fairness and trust.

Once the code was complete, he launched the site, although he had no idea what type of things people might want to sell and buy. As an experiment, he advertised his broken laser pointer for sale and to his surprise, found a buyer who was interested in broken ones. Pierre picked a handful of product categories including computer hardware and software, antiques, books and comics and users listed and viewed items and placed bids.

As he intended to offer the service for free, it was imperative that he kept his overheads as low as possible. To this end, he ran the site from his home, paying $30 a month to his internet service provider. He also decided to register the business, aiming to call it Echo Bay Technology as he thought the name 'sounded cool.' But when he tried to register it, he found it had already been taken by a Canadian mining company, so he chose the next closest name by shortening it to eBay.

The site quickly gathered momentum with virtually no publicity, and people began listing and buying all manner of goods. Pierre had eschewed advertising, PR and deals with other sites to boost traffic in favour of generating awareness by word of mouth. He posted his own announcements about the site with online newsgroups to attract attention. This had the desired effect as both computer geeks and those in search of a bargain emailed each other with details of the site. Towards the end of 1995, however, Pierre's internet service provider decided to charge him $250 a month to use the service, as it perceived that the sheer volume of traffic to the site was putting a strain on its system. It marked a turning point for Pierre and was the moment he decided to turn his hobby into a business.

'That's when I said, "You know, this is kind of a fun hobby, but $250 a month is a lot of money,"' he recalled in *The Perfect Store*. From the start, Pierre had designed the site to collect a small fee based on each sale. Implementing this charge provided him with the necessary money to fund overheads and expand the business. He decided to charge 5% of the sale price for items below $25 and 2.5% for items above this. This model was altered later to include a charge for listing items.

Pierre wanted, above all, to promote the idea of a community on the web, one which was built on fairness and trust

Going for growth

The fees added up to more than his current salary so it was an easy decision to quit his job and devote his full attention and time to the site. In June 1996, with the site recording more than $10,000 in revenues for that month and 41,000 registered users, Pierre hired his first employee, Jeff Skoll, who had previously been involved in two hi-tech startups. He also set up feedback facilities on the site to enhance the buying and selling process, which reinforced his original mission of creating a trusted community. A year later, eBay was attracting more consumers than any other online site.

'By building a simple system, with just a few guiding principles, eBay was open to organic growth – it could achieve a certain degree of self-organisation', Pierre said in one interview.

HOW **THEY** STARTED

In 1997, with the business growing at a phenomenal rate, Pierre invested substantially in advertising for the first time and helped design what has now become the business' iconic logo. The year marked another milestone as the one millionth item was sold on eBay – a toy version of *Sesame Street*'s Big Bird. By 1998, the site was making a name for itself as the place to trade for Beanie Babies – stuffed animals that were fast becoming a collector's item.

Fortune continued to favour Pierre's sense of timing. Towards the end of 1997 and throughout 1998, business communities around the world were experiencing the dotcom boom, and anything and everything online was attractive to investors and consumers alike. Pierre recognised that the business was becoming too big for him alone to handle, and the time was right to seek outside help and expertise. He had already fulfilled several roles, including those of chief financial officer, president and chief executive officer (CEO), as well as being chairman of the board.

Pierre decided to seek outside funding and sold a 22% stake in the business to venture capitalists Benchmark Capital in return for a $6.7m (which is £4.7m or $8.4m today) injection of finance, which some reports have suggested was the most lucrative investment ever made in Silicon Valley. Benchmark began the search for an experienced management team and new recruits included Margaret (Meg) Whitman, a Harvard Business School graduate who had previously worked for Disney. She took over the role of president and CEO, while Pierre remained as chairman. Meg poached senior executives from the likes of PepsiCo and Disney, helped to take the company public in 1998, and presided over a big investment in advertising.

The initial public offering was a phenomenal success and provided funds for further expansion. Pierre and Meg watched the shares jump from $18 to $50 apiece in a matter of minutes, and within two months of listing, shares had reached $100 apiece. By early 1999, Benchmark's stake was worth $2.5bn, equating to a staggering return of 50,000%. After a secondary offering, eBay's valuation peaked at $26bn (£16bn).

Teething troubles

Rapid growth came at a price, however. In June 1999, following a site redesign, eBay suffered a number of breakdowns in its service, with one lasting 22 hours. This had a severe impact on consumer interaction with the site and knocked more than $8 off the price of its shares. Further outages occurred and company revenues took a severe hit – according to reports at the time, the service interruptions cost eBay $3.9m of its second-quarter revenues, as it refunded listing fees and granted extensions on auctions.

At the time, the 22-hour outage was one of the worst internet crashes in history and a backlash quickly ensured as users wasted no time registering their complaints on an

EBAY'S WELL-KNOWN BRIGHT SIGNAGE OUTSIDE ITS HEADQUARTERS IN SAN JOSE, CALIFORNIA

internet newsgroup dedicated to the site. Others raised questions about the robustness of the technology.

Keeping the customer foremost in mind had always been Pierre's aim and he set about reassuring customers about the quality of the service. Staff worked round the clock to address technical problems and eBay made 10,000 phone calls to the site's top users, alerting them to the problems, apologising and ensuring that everything possible was being done to get the site back up and running.

A few users however, began turning to other sites that were giving eBay a run for its money with their own versions of online auctions, most notably search engine Yahoo! and online retailer Amazon. The latter had launched online auctions in March 1999, with a model similar to eBay's, including a commission on sales and a rating and feedback system. Competition however, appeared to be a good thing as eBay beefed up its services in response. It expanded the range of products on offer, strived to improve the buying and selling process and set its sights on global growth.

Worldwide expansion

In 1999, eBay launched sites in the UK, Australia, Germany and Canada and Pierre and Meg also implemented a strategy that involved selling more expensive goods on the site. This entailed launching a series of regional sites, which they believed would facilitate the sale of larger items that would be cumbersome and expensive to shift, such as vehicles. eBay also went on the acquisition trail and a year later, bought online retailer half.com, which allowed users to buy goods directly without going through an auction.

By 2001, eBay had added Ireland, Italy, Korea, New Zealand, Singapore, Japan and Switzerland to its portfolio of international sites and user numbers had swelled to 42 million. Such rapid expansion was an impressive feat in itself, but it was also achieved against a background of doom and gloom in the dotcom community. Many internet businesses had sought a public listing and seen their shares and valuations soar in the same vein as eBay's, but by 2001, it was a different story altogether as one online business after another went bust.

> *Such rapid expansion was an impressive feat in itself, but it was also achieved against a background of doom and gloom in the dotcom community*

eBay didn't have it all its own way however, as the Asian market proved difficult to crack. By 2002, it had pulled the plug on its operations in Japan, two years after launch, admitting that it was struggling to make inroads in a market where competitors such as Yahoo! Japan had a well-established auction model. According to reports, eBay was only able to offer 25,000 products on its Japanese site, while Yahoo! Japan had close to 3.5 million items. But as one door closed, another one opened – eBay's entrepreneurial spirit and appetite for global challenges hadn't been dampened in the slightest, and it set its sights instead on China, buying a third of Eachnet.com, the country's leading online auction site.

It also looked at ways of improving its services and in 2002, it bought electronic payment system PayPal in a deal valued at $1.5bn. PayPal was the leading player in the online payments market and eBay's own bespoke payment system, Billpoint, had failed to dent PayPal's market share. It seemed to make sense teaming up with a winning formula and Meg hoped the acquisition would help to speed up the site's existing payment processes.

In 2004, eBay introduced the 'Buy it now' functionality, enabling sellers to bypass the auction process and sell immediately to consumers. A year later, it launched a business and industrial category, offering items from the industrial surplus business. Its most surprising move was to come a year later, with the acquisition of internet telephony provider Skype in October 2005, at a cost of around $2.6bn (which is £1.5bn or $2.7bn today). At the time, eBay said it planned to integrate Skype with its auction website to smooth the sales process in those categories that called for better channels of communication, such as used cars and high-end collectibles. The deal also enabled eBay to extend its reach globally, accessing an audience in Europe and Asia, areas where it had so far failed to gain a strong foothold.

Survival of the fittest

While many analysts questioned the logic behind the eBay-Skype deal, and others said eBay had paid too much, one thing was clear: by the time it celebrated its 10th anniversary in 2005, eBay had proved itself many times over as an internet business that was here to stay. It had peaked at the time of the dotcom boom and survived while other high-profile, venture capital-backed brands such as Boo.com, clickmango and WebVan had disappeared altogether.

Today, more than seven million new items are listed on eBay each day and more than 112 million items are available at any given time

While its auction foray into China ultimately proved unsuccessful (it closed the website at the end of 2006 and entered instead into a joint venture run by a Chinese internet company), eBay had more success with Skype. In 2007, Meg said Skype had more customers in China than in the USA and the growth rate in China is faster than anywhere else.

Fittingly for an internet business, eBay has not been slow to capitalise on other technology opportunities, offering a WAP site, SMS alerts and blogs. It has also diversified its services further, offering Best of eBay, a site dedicated to finding the most unusual items advertised and eBay Pulse, which provides information on popular search terms and most-watched items.

More recently the company has branched out into other international markets and expanded its auctions business into event ticketing and comparison shopping, while navigating its fair share of challenges. The overall growth of its core auctions business has slowed, there have been numerous incidents of fraud carried out on the site and it has faced intense competition from search engine giant Google, which has squared up to PayPal by launching Checkout, its own online payment system. Amazon too has begun to attract independent sellers, the core of eBay's business.

Where are they now?

Today, more than seven million new items are listed on eBay each day and more than 112 million items are available at any given time. Its three biggest markets are the USA, the UK and Germany. Pierre's personal wealth meanwhile is estimated to be around £4.5bn ($8bn) and he was listed at number 120 in the *Forbes* 2008 list of the world's billionaires. He remains chairman of eBay but has kept himself busy with other ventures, such as

HOW **THEY** STARTED

THE INSIDE OF EBAY'S HEAD QUARTERS

Omidyar Network, a philanthropic investment firm. He is also a director of Meetup, a local community site in which he has an investment.

In April 2008, Meg stepped down as CEO, and was succeeded by John Donahoe, president of eBay's Marketplaces division. Business on the global front looks promising, with 54% of revenues coming from international markets, compared to 47% two years ago. Part of the site's success has also been down to its ability to innovate as well as to adapt, a vision that has been with the company from the very beginning, as Pierre explained in an interview in 2000:

'What eBay did was create a new market, one that wasn't really there before. We've had to evolve our strategies and policies from what I built in the beginning, which was a self-policing community of people, to one where we take a more active role in trying to help identify the bad actors,' he said.

This still holds true today. The site has recently introduced new measures to make its auctions and fixed-price listings easier to use, revamped its feedback mechanisms and strengthened its anti-fraud provisions in a bid to make eBay a safer place in which to trade.

Google

SEARCHING FOR SUCCESS

Founders: **Sergey Brin and Larry Page**

Age of founders at start: **24 and 25**

Background: **Stanford PhD computer science students**

Year of foundation: **1998**

Business type: **Search engine**

Countries now trading in: **Worldwide**

Income: **$4.2bn (£2.1bn) (2007)**

HOW **THEY** STARTED

G oogle. We all know its name and use its website probably more than any other. We also know that it is extremely successful and that its founders have become billionaires. Yet amazingly, 10 years ago, almost none of us had heard of it, let alone used it. Its growth has been more substantial than even most of the businesses described in this book, but also faster than any.

The birth of PageRank

Google hasn't always been such a goldmine. In fact, when they started, Google's co-founders Larry Page and Sergey Brin weren't even sure how their site would make money.

The pair met at Stanford University in the spring of 1995, where they were both enrolled on its prestigious PhD computer science programme. Located in Silicon Valley, Stanford had already spawned some of the world's most successful technology companies, such as Hewlett-Packard and Sun Microsystems, and the academic environment encouraged risk taking and entrepreneurship. Its office of technology licensing offered technologists resources, advice and assistance with the patent process to help its students commercialise their research projects in return for a stake in the businesses. It was also a stone's throw from Sand Hill Road, home to some of the USA's most successful venture capital firms.

Sergey and Larry had both grown up surrounded by science and technology. Larry's father was one of the first ever recipients of a computer science degree from the University of Michigan. His mother was a database consultant with a master's in computer science.

GOOGLE'S FOUNDERS SERGEY AND LARRY

Sergey was born in Moscow and came to the USA when his parents moved there; his mother was a scientist at NASA and his father a maths lecturer at the University of Maryland. Sergey had completed his BSc in mathematics and computer science at the University of Maryland by the age of 19; while Larry had built a working inkjet printer out of Lego at high school. So by the time they met both were highly accustomed to the use of computers and how they worked. They struck up a strong friendship at Stanford, fuelled greatly by their shared love of academic debate and discourse.

At the time, several rudimentary search tools existed, but a search on one of them would generally yield thousands of results, which were not ranked in any order of relevance. Fellow Stanford PhD students Jerry Yang and David Filo had developed Yahoo! to tackle the problem, but they employed a team of editors to assemble a web directory, and were already struggling to keep up with the mushrooming worldwide web. Convinced there was a better way, Sergey, an expert in extracting information from vast amounts of data, joined forces with Larry, who was studying the leading search engine Alta Vista. Never short of ambition, Larry had set out to download the entire web onto his PC to study the relevance of web links, which Alta Vista didn't appear to be taking into account. The project took far longer than expected and cost the computer science department around $20,000 (£12,000) every time they sent out a crawler programme to capture online data – but the effort was definitely worth it.

Never short of ambition, Larry had set out to download the entire web onto his PC to study the relevance of web links

They concluded that the number of links pointing to a site was a measure of its popularity. Furthermore, they decided that links could be weighted. For instance, if the BBC links to your website (which receives high volumes of traffic and has many links pointing to itself), this is worth more than a link from a less-popular site. Naming it after himself, he called the algorithm he developed to establish this pecking order PageRank. By adding this to traditional search methods – which matched keywords on pages with those in the search terms – the pair devised a search engine that produced results that were highly accurate and relevant to the user's request. Google was conceived.

Looking for a buyer

The founders did not set out to build a business. Coming from backgrounds where academia was revered, they were more excited to have stumbled across the basis of a killer thesis. They developed a prototype of their search engine, called BackRub, which was renamed Google in 1997. The term was a play on the word googol, a mathematical term for one followed by 100 zeros, and it represented the vast amounts of data on the web. Working day-in, day-out from a room on campus, the founders unleashed their creation on Stanford's student body via the university's intranet. Its popularity among this information-hungry population soared through word-of-mouth recommendations, as users quickly discovered how much faster and more relevant its search results were.

Not wanting to get too distracted from their academic pursuits, but certain they had created something far superior to anything else available at the time, they attempted to sell their technology to Excite, Yahoo! and the then market leader Alta Vista for up to $1m before patenting it. Amazingly, each company passed up on the opportunity. Search did not present any obvious revenue-generating opportunities and Google's goal to produce results in a split second did not make it an ideal space for advertisers. Feeling passionately that they had developed something that people truly needed, Sergey and Larry were left with no choice but to take Yahoo! co-founder David Filo's advice and take Google to market themselves.

By amassing email feedback from their academic peers, they refined their offering before seeking funding to make it scalable. In August 1998, they met private investor Andy Bechtolsheim, a co-founder of Sun Microsystems who had sold another business to Cisco for hundreds of millions of dollars. Despite the lack of a clear business model, Bechtolsheim was so taken with the idea that he wrote out a cheque to Google Inc for $100,000 (£60,000) on the spot, compelling Sergey and Larry to incorporate the company. Google was born.

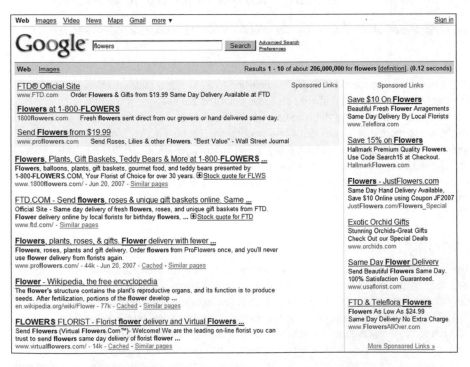

THE VERY WELL-KNOWN GOOGLE SCREEN, TOP OF ALL SEARCH ENGINES

Scaling it up

Bechtolsheim was particularly impressed with their plans to rely solely on the strength of their product and word-of-mouth recommendations to market the brand, instead of blowing huge sums on advertising. Instead, they planned to invest in IT as no other company had done before. From the offset, Sergey and Larry had been extremely efficient in their use of computers. They were downloading, indexing and searching the internet using a network of off-the-shelf PCs which they had custom built and linked together themselves. On these computers ran the software and algorithms they had also designed to crawl through and rank web pages. The intention was to continue with this strategy, scaling it up cost-effectively by adding more and more PCs to the network to ensure their lightning-fast search results kept up with the growing number of websites and users.

Google's stated mission is 'to organise the world's information and make it universally accessible and useful'

Following Bechtolsheim's endorsement, several friends and family members also backed the pair, who were able to raise a total of $1m (600,000). After running their operations from a garage for a while, where they hired their first staff member, the duo moved into offices on Palo Alto in 1999. A mention in *PC Magazine*'s top 100 websites created a huge surge in user numbers, and before long, Google was dealing with upwards of 500,000 searches each day.

However, struggling to maintain the level of IT investment they needed to keep up with these growing numbers, they were forced to seek further backing before long. Luckily for them, the economic climate worked in their favour. Google's story is set against the backdrop of the dotcom rise (and subsequent fall). Following the buzz created by the stock market flotation of internet browser producer Netscape in 1995, which valued the company at $3bn after the first day of trading, Wall Street stockbrokers were on the prowl for more internet success stories.

In 1999, Google closed a deal with two of the world's most prestigious venture capital firms (VCs), both based on Sand Hill Road, California: Sequoia Capital, which had backed Yahoo!, and Kleiner Perkins, which had backed Amazon, and many others. In an unprecedented move, the renowned VCs agreed to invest equally in Google, with neither having a controlling interest. They were so eager to back the search pioneer while they had the chance (despite it still having no successful business model) that each firm stumped up $12.5m (£7.5m), while Sergey and Larry remained in sole charge of the company they had created – a non-negotiable condition for them.

HOW **THEY** STARTED

Going global

Following the buzz this created, Google experienced a major growth spurt. They continued with their method of custom-building server racks using parts from low-cost PCs and stacking them one on top of the other, getting maximum value per square foot in their data centres. At this stage, their business model was to earn income by licensing their search technology to other partners. This wasn't bringing in anything like sufficient revenue, so they began to consider other ways to turn their growing search engine into a sustainable business.

They were initially hesitant to allow advertisers onto the site because they worried that users would doubt the search results' impartiality – and Sergey and Larry remained resolute that they would never allow companies to pay to rank more highly, as other search engines had done. They came up with a compromise which was to revolutionise not only their own business, but also their competitors' and, no less, the world's advertising industry. Their idea was that whenever someone searched for a topic, they would display small text adverts relevant to the subject of the search alongside the more prominent 'natural search engine results'.

Sergey and Larry remained resolute that they would never allow companies to pay to rank more highly ... they came up with a compromise which was to revolutionise the worlds advertising industry

This soon evolved into the current pay-per-click model, whereby Google would earn money whenever a user clicked on one of these 'sponsored links'. The rate paid per click was set by the advertiser in a fair, automated online auction process. This worked spectacularly well for several reasons: it was extremely simple and quick for an advertiser to set up; it could be tested for a tiny investment – far smaller than any other advertising method; it enabled advertisers to present their message to a very highly targeted and hungry audience; it was free unless someone clicked on the advertiser's advert; it was easy to measure how successful it was; and above all, it worked. Advertisers got excellent results from people clicking on their ads.

In 2000, the founders hired Dr Eric Schmidt as chief executive to take over the day-to-day running of the business. Although Sergey and Larry were hesitant at first through fear of losing control of the company they had created (this was a condition of their investment that they had reluctantly agreed to) Schmidt's appointment proved to be extremely successful. In particular, his business expertise played a key role in Google's overseas expansion. One of the first things he noticed was that, while 60% of its searches came from outside the USA, just

5% of ad revenues came from overseas advertisers. While the searches had been available in foreign languages for some time and the business was truly serving a global audience, it had yet to make money from this. Under Schmidt's supervision, sales offices were duly established in London, Hamburg, Tokyo and Toronto. Revenue soared.

Google's stated mission is 'to organise the world's information and make it universally accessible and useful'. Hardly a modest ambition! As its revenue grew, it started adding new services to deliver more of this mission. By 2004 in addition to the core search engine, it offered Google Images, a huge library of searchable images, and Google News, a service that aggregated stories on any particular subject from around the world, and introduced Gmail, a web-based email service.

Going public

In 2004, the founders reluctantly listed the search engine on the Nasdaq Stock Exchange, raising $1.2bn (£600m). But going public was actually the last thing Sergey and Larry wanted to do. Apart from the fact that their independence had helped them weather the dotcom storm, they were extremely reluctant to make their financial information available to competitors. Up until 2004, analysts had grossly underestimated just how big the search giant had become, and the last thing Google wanted was for the world to know how much money they were making, or more information on how they were making it. However, they had become so big that US law required them to disclose their financial information. Given that they would have to spill the beans anyway, they felt it prudent to take the company public, and give their early employees and investors a tangible return.

No other company has created such phenomenal influence, profit and wealth in such a short time

But shortly before its initial public offering (IPO), a number of factors coincided to bring down Google's share price. Firstly, the company had to deal with backlash from rival Overture, a subsidiary of its largest competitor, Yahoo!. Overture pioneered the idea of selling ads to accompany search results using a pay-per-click model, and accused Google of infringing its patents. Conscious of the negative affect the ongoing legal battle was having in the run up to its stock market debut, Google's founders gave Yahoo! 2.7 million shares in an out of court settlement.

Secondly, its recent entry into the email market with Gmail had been steeped in controversy. The founders had sought to offer a service that was far better than anything else out there. Using their search technology, you could easily search for and find a stored message using Gmail and they offered what was then a colossal one gigabyte of space with an account. However, their plans to make money through contextual ads, which were generated by scanning messages and matching ads to keywords, were slated by privacy bodies.

The combination of factors meant that Google's IPO valued shares at just $85 (£43) each. But this didn't last for long. Despite these setbacks, Google's share price rose to $100 by the end of the first day of trading, valuing the company at $23.1bn (£11.5bn). As with many new companies in Silicon Valley, many of Google's early employees had been given share options (instead of high salaries, which helped keep the young business' costs down while they were trying to become profitable) which made them millionaires when the company went public.

Part of Google's phenomenal growth has come from a scheme it created called AdSense. This allows other websites to install a Google search box on their site; when users click on the contextual ads that Google supplies alongside the results, the partner website earns some of the fee advertisers pay to Google. AdSense has been enormously popular with other websites, even including giants such as AOL and the *New York Times*. AdSense is typical of Google's progressive approach, and its belief that working alongside competitors can grow the market for all.

Where are they now?

Two months after the IPO, Google's share price hit $135 (£68). Since then it has risen substantially as the company's revenue and profits have grown; the share price currently stands at $528. Its market capitalisation (the current value of all its shares) is a staggering $165.87bn (£89bn) (correct at time of writing). When its stock value exceeded $700 a share in November 2007, Google became the fifth largest listed company in the USA.

TECHNICIANS HARD AT WORK IN THE GOOGLE OFFICE

Furthermore, Google's triumphant revenue and profit figures in the first quarter of 2008 have quashed rumours that it faced a slump in advertising income in 2007. At the height of its success in 2007, shares in Google were being sold for $741.80 (£370), but its price began to tumble amid fears that its ad revenue was falling (newspapers reported fewer people were clicking on its ads). But, true to form, Google laid waste to those claims when it brought home $1.3bn (£700m) profit between January and March 2008, from a turnover of $5.1bn (£2.7bn). Its presence online has become so mighty that IT giant Microsoft, keen to extend its reach in online search, recently attempted to buy Yahoo! for $44.6bn. Google and Microsoft continue to battle it out to entice the world's brightest technology engineers.

Google has used its success to make a number of significant acquisitions. Examples include its $1.65bn purchase of user video-clip phenomenon YouTube in October 2006 and online advertising network Doubleclick in April 2007, which it bought for $3bn, lengthening its reach into the display advertising market on the web.

Sergey and Larry moved to their Mountain View headquarters, in California, in 2004 and that is where the company remains to this day. The company's founding principles have also played a key part in the company's success, not least the founders' determination to make Google a great place to work. Its motto, 'don't be evil', is world famous, as is the award-winning culture that Sergey and Larry have fostered. On site at its Mountain View headquarters, staff can make use of a wide range of facilities, including pool tables, swimming pools and volley ball courts, as well as being well fed with free gourmet food. They receive more than 1,300 job applications every week.

The founders are still keen to solve some of the world's great problems. New products such as Google Earth, a service that enables users to hone in on any part of the globe using satellite imagery, have continued to wow its users. A project to map human genes is currently underway. Engineers are given 20% of their time where they are actively encouraged to work on their own projects. Both Google News and Froogle, an online shopping service, are the result of this initiative. It now has sales offices all over the world and this culture of creativity pervades them all.

Its motto, 'don't be evil', is world famous, as is the award-winning culture that Sergey and Larry have fostered

Google's website now processes hundreds of millions of searches every day. Google's homepage has retained its design simplicity and has not tried to use it for even more advertisements – despite the fact that it could potentially be a source of considerable extra income. As a result, it loads quickly, improving the customer experience. Likewise it has steered clear of flash features and other such things that would slow it down. It is estimated that Google's network now consists of more than 400,000 servers, a computing power unmatched by any other company. Its employees still assemble and customise the PCs the company uses to carry out its searches. No enterprise has more computing power than Google. No other company in history has achieved such brand awareness without spending heavily on advertising and marketing and no other company has created such phenomenal influence, profit and wealth in such a short time.

With thanks to the following contributing authors:

adidas	Kim Benjamin
Billabong	Jon Card
Cloudy Bay	Beth Bishop
The Coca-Cola Company	Beth Bishop
Green & Black's	Michelle Rosenberg
KFC	Kim Benjamin
Pizza Hut	Kim Benjamin
Dyson	James Hurley and Beth Bishop
Volvo Cars	Stephanie Welstead
Dorling Kindersley	Beth Bishop
Lonely Planet	Emma Haslett
IKEA	Michelle Rosenberg
Hilton Hotels	Holly Ivins
Apple	Emma Haslett
BlackBerry (RIM)	Stephanie Welstead
Nintendo	Jon Card
Nokia	Michelle Rosenberg
Sony	Kim Benjamin
Bebo	Matt Thomas and Beth Bishop
eBay	Kim Benjamin
Google	Stephanie Welstead

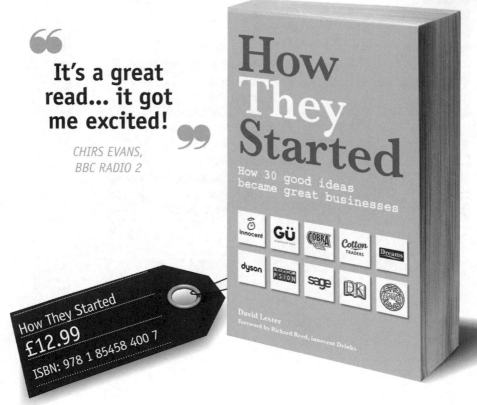

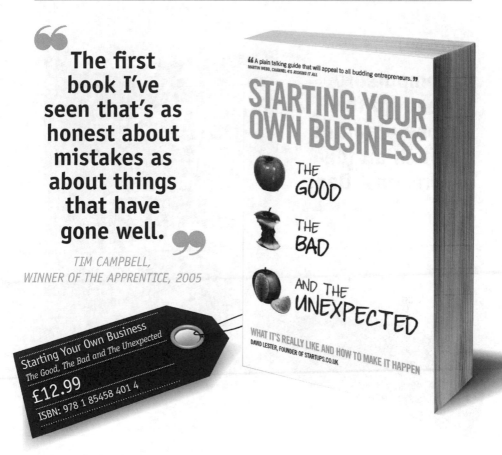

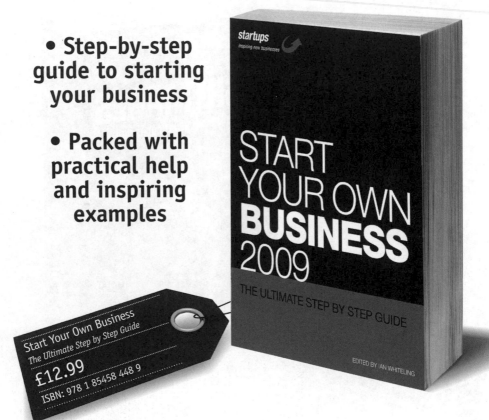

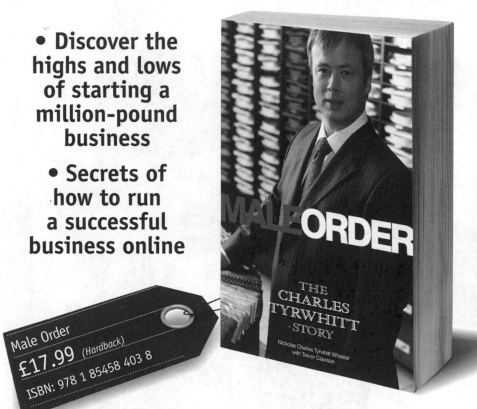